D0823519

1998

The Fearless DINER

TRAVEL TIPS *and* **WISDOM** *for* **EATING** *around the* **WORLD**

The Fearless DINER

TRAVEL TIPS *and* WISDOM *for* EATING *around the* WORLD

BY RICHARD STERLING

Travelers' Tales, Inc.
San Francisco, California

Distributed by
O'Reilly and Associates
101 Morris Street, Sebastopol, CA 95472

The Fearless Diner: Travel Tips and Wisdom for Eating Around the World
By Richard Sterling

Copyright ©1998 Travelers' Tales, Inc. All rights reserved.
Printed in Canada

Travelers' Tales and Travelers' Tales Guides are trademarks of
Travelers' Tales, Inc.

Cover design by Kathryn Heflin
Interior design by Susan Bailey
*Cover illustration: © Michael Surles, full watercolor painting of world
   landscapes*
Cover photograph: © Garret Culhane

Printing History
March 1998:   First Edition

To Bruce and Paul Harmon,
a couple of Fearless Ones.

ISBN: 1-885-211-22-8

TABLE OF CONTENTS

—

$\mathcal{I}$NTRODUCTION

There is in some few men of every land a special hunger, one
which will make them forgo the safe pleasures of their own beds
and tables, one which initiates them into that most mysterious
and ruthless sect: the Adventurers.

—Mary (M.F.K.) Fisher

———

I WAS ON MY WAY to circumnavigate the globe a few
years ago, to literally eat my way around the world. It was
my gustatory goal for that year. I stopped in Bangkok to
visit Sven Krause, executive chef of the Celadon restaurant
in the Beaufort Sukhothai Hotel. He took me into the inner
sanctum of the Celadon's kitchen, where he dared me any
half-dozen dishes just to prove he could make them and
make them quickly. It was no contest. Within minutes he
presented me with a Thai feast. As I munched each delec-
table dish, I asked him to tell me his most unusual cooking experience.

"You won't believe it," he said.

"Try me," I said, feeling a tug of intuition about the tale
he was going to relate.

"I was working in Saudi Arabia," he continued. "There
was a wedding of some sheik or other. And you won't
believe what they wanted me to cook."

I knew in my gut, in my gastronomic soul, that what I
had long hoped was true. That it wasn't just some wild traveler's tale designed to stir the imagination and not the pot.
The ultimate cookout was a reality. The only thing that
could possibly be greater would be to spit-roast a giant
squid. My wildest culinary dream could come true. Sven,
Allah bless him and may his tribe increase, had done it.

"I tell you no lie," he went on, sipping a cold one. "They wanted camel. I roasted a whole camel on a spit."

"Yes!" I cried. "Tell me everything." And he did. He told me how he stuffed the camel with six sheep, stuffed the sheep with chickens, and the chickens with fish. He told me how it took 24 hours to cook, and that he served it on a silver platter in the shape of a recumbent camel. He related how the tribesmen who were the sheik's guests then attacked it with their knives en masse, feasted with their bare hands, and ate the meat down to the ivory.

"Sven, I'm going to Rajasthan. There lives the largest camel herd in the world. I intend to roast me one of them. I'll give a great feast to the Rajputs. I'll invite all the local potentates and nabobs and other poobahs. Tell 'em to bring their families and harems and seventh sons. This is the Holy Grail for me, Sven. This is my golden fleece, my windmill to topple. Bless me, Sven, you who have done this mighty deed."

"You'll need more than my blessing," he said. "You'll need a crack team to help you, the luck of the Irish, and a strong stomach. The best part is the loin."

"I've always heard it was the hump."

"Forget the hump. It's nothing but bone and fat. And shave the hair off the chest and under his tail. That's the fleecy part. After you eat him, you have someone weave you a nice coat of him."

"Thanks, Sven. Thanks for saving my dream. I was beginning to despair."

"Good luck, Richard. You're going to need it."

That was the last I saw of Sven. But I had his blessing and his recipe for whole roast camel. I was ready to go forth.

Are you?

I
THE GREAT GASTRONOMICAL GLOBE

I have eaten your bread and salt,
I have drunk your water and wine.
The deaths Ye died I have watched beside
And the lives Ye led were mine.
- *Rudyard Kipling*

───────

WELCOME TO THE TABLES OF THE WORLD. As you know, many of us travel, in large part, to eat. And the many conventional guidebooks give us some aid in that pursuit. But what of Us, the Adventure Eaters, we visceral souls who literally consume culture, put the world on a plate, and gobble up the road?

If you are reading this, you are like me, a person of the senses. And I think you will agree with the proposition that humanity is revealed through cuisine, through the customs and traditions and practices of food production, preparation, and consumption, just as surely as it is through any other art or social activity.

The Fearless Diner takes his or her place in a long and unbroken tradition of epic journeys, from hunting mastodon to blazing the spice routes.

Homer, in *The Odyssey*, often breaks his narrative to tell how the Greek heroes laid down their arms and feasted during their wars and travels, how they chased down goats, made wine, carved meat, and consumed "baskets of dainties." The message for us is that feasting and adventuring are inextricably intertwined; cuisine is an integral part of the landscape, a character in the tale of your own adventure. And furthermore, it's just plain fun to eat your way around the world. It's fun to plan culinary journeys, it's fun to discover new tastes and to be invited into new kitchens. And it's fun to dine on the edge.

Too often, people take the subject of food out of its context and treat it as some discreet activity unconnected to real life. Or they insist that it be kept in a realm of gentility, refinement, at a far remove from daily life, adventurous life, or life in the raw and on the road. But not the Fearless Diners.

The Fearless Diners do not pluck the Muse of Cuisine from the continuum of the life in which She resides. And She resides not only at the tables of the refined, the wealthy, and the well-scrubbed, She thrives everywhere. I've chased Her down back streets and dark alleys, and up the wealthy avenues of capital cities. She's led me through asphalt jungles and cultural deserts, into European five-star restaurants, Mexican fugitives' campsites, Moghul palaces, and Chinese fishermen's shacks. I've even found Her lounging in the rooftop kitchen of a Philippine whorehouse.

She's everywhere. This muse has guts, She does not shy away. I can tell you that She is wherever people dine fearlessly. She will even attend runaway boys if they know a good dinner when they find it. As in the case of Tom Sawyer and his friends feasting on an island in the Mississippi: "It seemed glorious sport to be feasting in that wild free way in the virgin forest…and they said they would never return to civilization."

Who are the Fearless Diners, and how is their way different from others? And just how fearless are they? They are as fearless as they need to be to satisfy desires on a given day in a shifting landscape of circumstance. One Fearless Diner's circumstance may take him to mountaintops or jungles; another's takes him across town. Fearlessness is not so much in what the diner dines upon, but how.

The Fearless Diner seeks a life of contrast, juxtaposition, complementary forces. In a word: antithesis. The Fearless believe that we cannot know a thing without knowing something of its opposite. We would not be aware of the light without experience of the dark. The Fearless Diner regards the ugly as a gift, because without it there could be no beauty. Pleasure can only be known in a life that knows pain. The Fearless Diner is a seeker and a knower of beauty and pleasure in a world of light.

A Fearless Diner may camp in some remote area, and char freshly caught meat over the open fire, then eat it plain with a rough red wine. Returning home, that same Fearless Diner, nostrils still full of woodsmoke, might dine in a place with a fancy name on truffles and champagne. And that's good fearless dining. A pair of Fearless Diners, in black tie and evening gown, may depart a fancy ball with their bellies full of caviar, then spend the rest of the night with sailors, off-duty cops, or illegal aliens, drinking from a brown paper bag—and still in formal attire! Or they may do something as simple as eat Chinese for breakfast, Indian for lunch, and Italian for dinner. The Fearless Diner could live on gruel, and serve the poor in some faraway mission, and still keep a nose for fine wine.

The Fearless Diner will not consider herself fully alive until she has grappled in some way with Death. The Fearless Diner loves to laugh, and so he never fears to cry. The Fearless Diners love a full belly, so never fear an empty one. They know that true satisfaction comes from longing.

Emptiness is prelude to fullness, dirt to cleanliness, and fatigue to blissful rest. In our travels, it isn't where we go and what we eat and drink, but how.

The wide world is shrinking, Fearless One. But there will always be kitchens and markets to explore; through gastronomic travel a whole new dimension of the globe awaits us. Those who know, or would know, the joy of seeing the world food first will find *The Fearless Diner* their best pocket companion. Bold Epicures will find here the tips and wisdom needed to feast with savages, break bread with kings, and get invited home to dinner: Indian table manners, which fork to start with at Maxim's, and the proper use of chopsticks; what's good/safe/politically correct to eat or do and what is taboo; how to find the best, make the best of the worst, avoid getting sick, and what to do if you can't help it.

This is your literary mess kit. Pack a toothbrush and go a' feasting.

Go fearlessly, but don't go blindly. Study the possibilities. Learn what might lay ahead in the Great Gastronomical World. Set gustatory goals! If you have it on good authority that the finest tea is to be had only in some far and difficult corner, go and find it. Make it your special quest. I would never counsel you to ignore the museums, theaters, historical sites, and pleasant diversions that can be found on a conventional itinerary in a given country. But with what, how, and in what spirit, does that country nourish itself? In societies where public feasting is important, where it is the occasion for love and lust (Rio), political settlement (New Guinea), or high purpose (Jerusalem), put the feast day on your calendar and go. Make it your pilgrimage. Want to have some fun? In Spain they have an annual tomato fight! Running with the bulls? Ha! It's nothing compared to the sheer lusty exuberance of a real live attack of killer tomatoes on a city-wide scale. It's better than a pie fight! Seek out the rare, the taboo. Learn to dine on the knife's edge.

Going home to Greece with my two truly American children, Zoe, 11, and Danny, 9, we headed for a village west of Patras called Tsoukaleakia. That is where Chrysanthi, my oldest and dearest friend, went back to her family's land, built a house, started an organic citrus farm, and now keeps honey bees. My children were anxious to arrive at the farm after ten days in Italy, eager for the taste that makes them Greek: yogurt. Real yogurt. Not non-fat or low-fat. Real yogurt with real Greek honey, not a commercial diet food. The taste of the smooth sweet yogurt with the wonderful honey lingers like the love they always feel at Chrysanthi's farm. They can be the coolest and hippest California kids, but when we are at the farm, and they eat the yogurt and honey, then once again they reconnect to my homeland, my Greekness, and theirs.

◆

Clio Tarazi, urban planner, Berkeley, California

II

ℐHE ℋOLY ℐRINITY
OF ℭUISINE

Tell me what you eat, and I will tell you what you are.
—*Jean Anthelme Brillat-Savarin*

IF YOU WOULD BE FEARLESS, and not foolish (I've been both and can do without the latter), be informed. How do we access the Great Gastronomical World and the people who live in it? Most often in one of two ways: as a visitor—in a restaurant, home, farm, winery, fishing boat, or other supplier of things consumable; or yourself in the role of cook or host. Traditional eating places are excellent venues for personal encounters and cultural exchanges. Any time you are a guest in the home is an opportunity to become a student. And it's a simple matter to arrange a meal in a restaurant to entertain new friends; or to prepare them a picnic, or even to go into their home and prepare your native fare for them.

And what sort of native fare will you encounter when you go forth? A quick glance at the map of contiguous cultures and a passing knowledge of the migrations of peoples will give a fair idea for just about any place on the globe. In my years of gastronomic journeys I have found that all the numerous and myriad expressions of the culinary art, whatever forms being practiced in any kitchen, can all trace their lineage back to at least one of the three great "schools" of cuisine. And those schools are, in order of age, Chinese, Indian, and European. Of course they have their regional styles and variations, hybrids and cross-cultural fusions, offshoots and influences, but all can be distilled to this Holy Trinity of Cuisine.

I, and you, O Fearless One, can recognize each school by its commonly used foods, cooking techniques, kitchen equipment, and, most tellingly, by its characteristic "Flavor Battery." This is what I have learned in countless culinary encounters to be that peculiar combination of seasoning ingredients that instantly sets one school apart from another. And it is the variations on the Flavor Battery that chiefly make for a school's regional differences, and its offshoots and influences.

C H I N A

For the People, food is Heaven.
—*Chinese proverb*

CHINA COMES TO ME IN DREAMS. I awake from them with a hunger not only for Chinese cookery, but for life, love, and adventure. On the streets of China, Taiwan, Hong Kong, or the Chinatowns found in a score of cities around the world, Chinese restaurants—and the Chinese-inspired restaurants of Vietnam, Thailand, Laos, and others—send their culinary siren songs wafting through the air, never letting me forget the Middle Kingdom or its gustatory descendants. They awaken a thousand sensual memories of the urgent fragrances of chile and garlic, the joyful orderly chaos of the clang and bang of cooking vessels, of steam billowing from little noodle shops, and of the taste of life itself being savored.

The Chinese Flavor Battery is dominated by fermented sauces: soy, fish, oyster. Soy is by far the most common and is used almost exclusively as a cooking ingredient, not a condiment, despite the fact that we see it on the tables of Chinese restaurants in the United States. I learned this by having numerous Chinese waiters elsewhere make faces at me when I called for the stuff. Soy sauce alone, however, does not Chinese cookery make. Stalking the streets of any Chinese city my nose will detect soy, ginger, green onion, and in savoring any Chinese dish my tongue encounters rice wine, sugar, salt, and pepper. In the regional variations on the theme of this culinary "fugue," you encounter garlic, sesame, peanuts, chile pepper, rice vinegar, anise, or five-spice (a blend of sweet spices).

The most significant variation is in the tropical regions and the southern areas of influence where the heady fish sauce becomes the predominant fermentation product, ginger gives way to lemon grass, and garlic replaces green onions. But even these changes keep to the basic flavor triad of fermented sauce, pungent spice, and the genus *Allium*. This is a constant in the countries most influenced by the Chinese school: Japan, Korea, Burma, Thailand, Laos, Cambodia, Vietnam, Indonesia, Philippines.

The quick cooking techniques common to China, stir-frying and steaming, were adopted long ago when the land was deforested and fuel became scarce. Hence, baking is almost unknown, stewing is rare, with braising somewhat less so. Common foods are the staples of rice in the south and noodles in the north, anything that grows in the ground, anything from the sea, and "anything with legs except a table and anything with wings except an airplane," as many a Chinese cook has said to me. The cooking medium is almost exclusively vegetable oil, and the wok is the common vessel.

Among the guiding principals are frugality and improvisation. China has suffered many a famine, and so wasting anything is much frowned upon. In time of scarcity, the cook must be able to make do with whatever is available. Thus, the Chinese became the most omnivorous people in the world. Boasting is bad form in China, but in Hong Kong they pick up Western habits. A chef at one of the floating restaurants told me one evening that he could make a feast of an old shoe if it were made of honest leather, "No Nike shoe from Chinese sweatshop." I believe him a little more than not, as I once dined very well in Taiwan on a dish of steamed cowhide.

Its history has caused the Chinese school to become not a canon of recipes to be followed without error, or always the same because your mother did it that way. It became a philosophy, a way of thinking and doing. It became imbued with the Chinese principal of Yin and Yang which argues that all things in the universe are either of one polarity or the other: hot/cold, male/female, wet/dry, light/dark, and so on. This extends to all things edible. Harmony in the universe requires balance of Yin and Yang, so the cook strives to balance colors, textures, aromas, and the five flavors of salt, sweet, bitter, sour, and hot (or spicy). As you can see, the Chinese are the original Fearless Diners.

The great riddle of Peking duck: do you eat the skin, meat, soup or all? The answer is nearly certainly that the Emperor and closest associates ate only the skin. Other courtiers would eat only the meat. The boiled bones were made into a soup for the lower classes. In democracies, one can safely have all three courses.

◆

Harry Rolnick, editor, Budapest

I know Chinese cooks who can go anywhere in the world, deal with any kind of food and, if they have only the basic elements of the Flavor Battery, produce what will be recognizably Chinese school. The only time I have seen a Chinese chef fail at this was during my military days when I gave the poor sod a package of C-rations and challenged him to make it good. I never did that again.

The Chinese are also great snackers and eaters of tid-bits. And most of the cultures in China's culinary orbit follow suit. One of the most fetching sub-genres of the Chinese school is in Laos, hard by China's southern border. I often dine at the central market in the capital city of Vientiane. There's a stall in the southeast corner run by a woman who has dubbed me "Mr. Beer" for my taste for the brew at breakfast. Yes, at breakfast! It's hot there, the food is salty, and I don't have to drive, think, or operate machinery. (By the way, this is something I do not do back home, nor do I want to.)

When I showed up one morning, Madam took one look at me, turned to her daughter, smiled and said, "Bia," and the daughter fetched a cold one. Madam then turned to making one of my favorites of the tropical South China school: Som Tam. It's a spicy, tangy salad made from juli-enned green papaya tossed with chile, garlic, lime, toma-toes, and fish sauce. Then it's pounded a bit in a large mor-tar to release all the flavors and juices. It's very cleansing on the palate and a perfect foil for rich sauces or grilled meats. As this was going on, I turned my eyes to Madam's supply of skewered chicken, pork, fish, and items I couldn't iden-tify. All had been previously grilled and needed only reheating on the charcoal brazier. I pointed to one in the shadowy corner that looked like the strips of marinated pork I had enjoyed on previous occasions, but as my good lady of the grill placed the skewer on the fire, I noticed lit-tle appendages on each piece of meat that looked rather like legs.

It occurred to me that what I had just ordered was tree

frogs on a stick, a common item of diet in that corner of the world. I wasn't too alarmed, as I'd enjoyed stuffed frogs for dinner only the night before. But for last night's entree, the heads, guts, and skins had all been removed and the frog had been stuffed with a delicious force meat, rolled in spices and fried in a rich oil. Tree frogs on a stick, though, come to the table unaltered except by fire.

I thought of changing my order, but nobody at the market spoke English and I no Lao. Also, by this time I had attracted a small crowd of goggle-eyed children who had apparently never seen a blue-eyed demon at table, and I didn't want to give a bad account of my country. Besides, rats and bats on a stick are also common here; I figured I was getting off easy with tree frogs.

Madam's daughter turned the little beasties once more, then deskewered them onto a plate and set them before me. Frogs I was prepared for, but what I got was chicken feet! Marinated, grilled, scratch-at-the-ground chicken feet. The heel and toe, claw, instep and ankle of the common barnyard chicken is esteemed a tasty treat throughout the Far East. I have even seen them offered in the snack bars of movie theaters in Taiwan. Right next to the M&Ms. I tell no lie.

I always knew that someday I would face this moment, but I never relished it. Funny, isn't it, that I who would eat anything should quake at the sight of chicken feet. I who have supped on soup made of ant larvae, quaffed bowls of blood, dined on dogs and chewed through the guts of animals unknown. Not that I am an indiscriminate eater, mind you. My food must be artfully prepared and presented with care. But I've long boasted that I would eat anything at least once.

And now my gastronomic bravado was coming home to roost. Madam set the Som Tam in front of me and her daughter brought forth sticky rice. Excellent Lao beer had been well-chilled and poured into a frozen mug that had been resting under pounds of ice as though in anticipation of my arrival. The wide-eyed children seemed to hold their breath as though the thought had occurred to them that the big, sweaty farang might prefer the profane feast of a tender child to the undisputed and civilized delicacy of chicken feet. Their watchful parents ogled sidelong.

I sniffed. The aroma of BBQ chicken was unmistakable. No toe-jam smells or athlete's-foot odors obtained. I looked closely at the curled digits and saw that few talons remained. Whether they had burned off on the grill or been extracted for herbal medicines I don't know. Once again I looked to the people watching me. They all bore expressions that seemed to say, "Go ahead, friend. It's good." With thoughts of foot fetishes ajumble in my mind, I lifted one to my mouth, and as the children gawked, I gnawed. Dare I say it was finger-lickin' good? It tasted better than anything I had ever bought from the Colonel. And all the people watching smiled, in a way that said I had just done a good thing.

Of course there isn't much meat on a hen's foot, or a cock's either for that matter. You might get two swallows if you're a lady; one for a gentleman or a rogue. They're like pickled pig's feet: you nibble them for their flavor, not their nourishment. They provide much gustatory satisfaction with virtually no calories.

TIPS

➤ After gnawing on tasty chicken feet, use the toenails to pick your teeth.

➤ Learn how to say, "Have you eaten?" in Chinese. It's the typical greeting.

- ➤ The Chinese verb "to eat" is synonymous with "to eat rice." The words "eat" and "rice" cannot be spoken of separately.

- ➤ Rice is considered the main food, all else on the table is dressing for the rice. Put a little meat or vegetable into your rice bowl, then eat some of both. Then repeat the procedure. To eat just the meat and vegetable, and ignore the rice, is considered boorish.

- ➤ *Dim Sum* (most Chinese would say *Yan Cha*, which means "drink tea") are little steamed or deep fried buns filled with savory ingredients and served with tea. They are popular as a snack or for breakfast or lunch, but no later. At a traditional *Dim Sum* restaurant the server will wheel a cart, rather like a tea trolley filled with a variety, to your table. Pick and choose what and how many you like. To order more tea, simply remove the lid from your pot.

- ➤ The traditional beverage at dinner is not tea or rice wine but a clear soup. Nowadays, beer and soda are becoming more common.

- ➤ Tea drinking can be an everyday act; and it can be a ritual, as at weddings, funerals, reunions. After an argument, a Chinese

> ___ \\\|//_ ___
>
> *Entering my hotel room in Kaoshung, Taiwan I found a thermos of plain hot water, but no tea. I soon learned that the Chinese drink plain hot water just like tea. I found it very relaxing late at night when tea would have kept me awake.*
>
> ◆
>
> *Lisa Millay, CPA, Seattle, Washington*

couple are more likely to take tea than "kiss 'n' make up." The Japanese tea ceremony is so full of meaning as to be a metaphor for life itself. Good guidebooks will help you navigate these waters of ritual country by country.

➤ At a Chinese table, fish is often served head, tail and all. The eyes are highly regarded by many. After the meat is eaten, just pick up the head and suck the eyes out. Tasty. Very tasty.

➤ At a Chinese banquet, pace yourself. No matter how much you've eaten, there will be more.

➤ The usual service is family-style. Rather than a prescribed suc-cession of courses, everything is brought to the table at once (unless everything won't fit).

In Chinese restaurants a dirty tablecloth means the food is great.

◆

Kit Snedaker, editor, Santa Monica, California

➤ If you are entertaining or being entertained, frequent toasts will be customary. Try to arrange for some-thing other than the damnable sorgum liquor, "Maotai."

GUSTATORY GOALS

➤ Chinese, particularly Cantonese, communities are found all over the world. If you're traveling, say, across Europe, dine in a Chinese restaurant in each country through which you pass. Note the influences of the host countries on the enduring Chinese school. This will not only be a good gustatory goal, it will help to ensure against your falling into a culinary rut, what with all the wine and cheese and such.

➤ Since the Chinese will eat anything, seek out the "anything." In Hong Kong, for instance, you can find restaurants that serve African game. In Singapore and Hong Kong, you can find restaurants where they will craft a meal to cure what ails you. Throughout the Chinese world, cooks prepare snake, lizard, lion heart. You name it, you can get it. Go get it! Try it once!

—— ∿ ——

I knew there would be toast after toast at the dinner to which we had been invited to mark my husband's and my farewell to China the night before we departed. Jet lag was going to be bad enough. A hangover I didn't want. I told my hosts that, as a Catholic, I had made a vow to St. Francis that I would eschew alcohol for a month if he would grant me an easy journey. They gave me nothing but tea. St. Francis will forgive me. Amen.

♦

Marie MacAlister, textile engineer, Vancouver, British Columbia

➤ Want a private cooking lesson? At a small or family-owned restaurant, arrange a dinner for friends. Whatever the price is, offer another ten percent to have the cook allow you to observe, and to explain the processes and techniques and ingredients. Take notes. At a hole-in-the-wall eatery, or a pushcart kitchen, you can do the same, and do it hands-on, for as little as a pack of cigarettes. This is how I originally learned to cook in Singapore and Taiwan. And the sight of a foreign devil dishing up Chinese fare to the Chinese always brought "interesting" responses.

> At the Shao Lin Temple grounds in Taipei, nighttime belongs to cooks and the Chinese opera. Pushcart kitchens appear at sundown, seemingly out of nowhere. By the time the stars are out, the opera is tuning up. Though eggs were often the only thing I could recognize among his ingredients, I always ended my evenings at the omelet man's cart. And so did She. At the time, She spoke no English, and I little Chinese. We could do little more than point, smile, laugh, share. We've been married now for ten years.
>
> ◆
>
> Elliot Anderson, investment banker, Anchorage, Alaska

ᴵNDIA

I shall appear as the ex-cook of King Virata, as I am
well versed in the culinary arts.

—Bhima to Yudhishthira on how he will live in disguise,
The Mahabarata

IN NO OTHER CUISINE have I encountered a flavor battery to match the complexity and variety of India. At its most basic it is known as *masala*, a word that means roughly, "mix," a combination of sweet and piquant spices. What we call curry is an English invention from the days of the Raj and is virtually non-existent in India proper. Whenever I have asked for it in India I've been met with blank stares or giggles. A typical *masala* might include clove, cinnamon, cardamom (the sweet) and coriander, cumin, black pepper (the piquant). Foods may be cooked with this mixture alone, but onions and turmeric are often added. Additions and variations on this theme are limited only by the taxonomy of the spice world.

I learned of this in a sudden cultural immersion, on my way to Jaisalmer, east of Pakistan, while retracing the spice routes that had brought the luxury of pepper and cloves to ancient Rome. It was our second day out on the Great Indian Desert and we were driving our camels hard, determined to reach the village of Samrau before dark. As we approached the village we came upon a goatherd who tended a flock of about twenty. His name was Naglaman. He was amazed to see three camel-mounted foreigners, and with grand gestures invited us to tea. As we dismounted he disappeared into a little shelter he had made of twigs and desert scrub, and reemerged with his "tea service," one battered old pot, two metal cups of different origins, and a couple of desert palm leaves. The leaves he tore into pieces, then folded expertly into conical cups, disposable and biodegradable.

Over tea mixed with wild honey and goat's milk I asked Prayag Singh, our interpreter, what we could expect for dinner in Samrau that night. I knew it wouldn't be camel, and I was hugely disappointed. When I had tried to purchase a camel calf the previous day and feast the whole village, I thought there would be rejoicing. But the people were scandalized. Since the Hindu desert folk have no cows to worship, they substitute camels as their sacred animal. It's okay to ride them, but not to eat them. Was my face red! And what would I tell Sven Krause?

"*Chapatis* for dinner tonight," Prayag said. *Chapatis* are unleavened flatbread made from wheat or, among the desert people, millet.

"Of course," I said, uninspired. "Anything else?"

"Oh yes. Vegetables."

"Just like the last one. Are the desert people vegetarians?"

"No, no. But they eat meat only on special occasions, because it is very dear."

"How dear? For instance, how much would one of these goats here cost? Unless they're sacred, or something."

I settled with Naglaman the goatherd on 400 rupees

(US$12.50 at the time) for his fattest kid, weighing about forty pounds. He was very pleased with the bargain until I said, "But I gotta have a receipt. It's a business expense." His smile faded when Prayag translated. "It's not that I don't trust you," I said. "It's just that I have to keep careful records or my publishers will complain."

"But, Sahib, I don't know how to write," he said, and looked at the ground.

"Oh. I see." I took out my pen and notebook and said, "I'll write it out for you and all you'll have to do is sign it." I wrote it out and handed it to him saying, "There. Just sign your name. Can you do that for me?"

He looked even lower, and lowly said, "I don't know how to write my name, Sahib."

I felt like I had just stripped the man naked and whipped him through the streets. Prayag was speaking to him softly in Marwati, his native tongue, when an idea came to me. "Naglaman," I said, "My great grandfather couldn't write either. But he would sign documents with his thumb. How about I ink your thumb with this pen and you sign the receipt that way?"

The idea that he, an illiterate, nomadic goatherd could actually sign an official document attesting to the transfer of foodstuff suddenly raised his spirits, pumped up his chest and put the smile back on his face. Raising my pen I said, "Let's have your thumb." He stuck it eagerly in my face. I inked it up good, making sure to cover it all, while he looked on with something approaching wonder. I then held the notebook for him and he painstakingly rolled his thumb onto the paper. Prayag wrote across the thumbprint, first in Marwati and then in English, "Naglaman: his mark." The goatherd was now an honorary member of the order of letters.

I tethered the goat to my camel and we mounted and

rode on into the village. Our arrival caused quite a stir, though a happy one. We were conducted to a shade tree to sit and relax while the village headman was summoned. A group of locals sat around us and we chatted with them through the voice of Prayag. One of them pointed to me and said something that caused them all to giggle. Prayag reported that the villager had pointed out that among the desert people the color of my turban was the traditional color for widows' weeds. The villager jokingly asked if I were a widow. I said, "No. But just like a widow, I have no husband." If any ice needed breaking, that did the trick.

Soon the headman arrived and we were formally welcomed, told where we might sleep if we cared to stay, and invited to share their dinner. All the while the people had been hungrily eyeing my goat, which my companions, Bruce and Paul, had nicknamed "Jimmy."

"Why Jimmy?" I asked.

"We call any animal we kill and eat Jimmy. We do a lot of hunting."

"I wish he could have been Jimmy the Camel. Prayag, say that everyone is invited to the feast of Jimmy. As long as they agree to teach me how to cook him in their traditional way."

When the goat had been slaughtered, and a man we had dubbed "Yellow Hat," for the color of his turban, had finished the butchering, he summoned me to follow him into an enclosure. From a wooden chest he took out his ingredients and through Prayag he spoke. "I'm cooking this goat in the way of all the desert people. We use the spices that the caravans have always carried, and the red chile powder. We grow the chile in Rajasthan and we use it all in Rajasthan. The caravans have never carried it because other people find it too full of fire."

Another man brought out flint and steel and tinder,

and while all the men watched in reverent silence, he kindled the fire. Yellow Hat poured what looked like a pint of red chile powder into a big brass bowl. I tasted it, and it was indeed full of fire. It wasn't habañero, but it was still powerful stuff. On top of that he poured half as much turmeric powder. Atop that half as much *garam masala,* then half as much salt. Over the mound he sprinkled a layer of sweet paprika. Then he mixed

I found it very easy to get invited home to dinner in India. You just have to chat somebody up about Indian cookery. It's even odds the person has a great cook in the family and is eager to prove it to you.

♦

Rod Johnson, biologist,
Peterville, Ohio

them all with his gnarly fingers. Into a pot over the fire he poured oil and when it was hot threw in a handful of fennel seeds and cooked them till they all popped. Then he stirred in his spice mixture with some water.

When the mix had simmered awhile, he added several pounds of cubed meat. But Jimmy's heart and testicles he laid on the bare coals of the cooking fire and toasted them to a burnt-rare condition. He and I shared them as an hors d'oeuvre. Cook's prerogative.

Since that instructive dinner with Yellow Hat I've often watched the Indian Flavor Battery further expanded by means of roasting, grinding, or frying the spices, mixing and matching, and combining them with tart fruits such as tamarind or lime. In the state of Kerala, I offered my hosts my precious demi of California white wine to the purpose. It was so successful that one of the hosts, publisher of the city magazine of Ernaculum, made me an Editor Emeritus. Spice mixtures are made on the spot, balancing not only their gustatory properties, but their Ayurvedic medicinal and religious properties, and with attention paid to proportion, order, and procedure. They aren't simply mixed in a jar and dumped on the food.

Common cooking techniques include slow frying and braising or simmering to produce a sauce. The *tandoor*, which produces the famous Tandoori Chicken, is referred to as an oven, but it operates at such high temperature (over 600 degrees Fahrenheit) that its effect is more like broiling. Cooking media are vegetable and mustard oils, and *ghee*, clarified butter that has been cooked long and slow to give it deeper flavor and better keeping quality.

Common foods are a wide range of wheat or millet flatbreads in the North, rice in the South, legumes of all kinds, especially lentils (*dahl*) and peas. Meat is more popular in the North and may be "curried" or *tandoori*. Coconut milk as a sauce base and the more fiery spices are common in the South. Yogurt is widely used throughout.

In ancient times Indians, especially the herdsmen of the North, were great meat eaters. For reasons on which we can only speculate (overpopulation, ill-managed land or livestock, religious changes, etc.), they began to turn

> *In a New Delhi restaurant, vegetarian, white tile, clean, spotless, modern, efficient, little tiny tables for stand-up eating. Little bits of everything to nuance the palette from boredom —spicy potatoes, soothing mild lentils, a soupy yogurt infused with cucumber to take down the temperature of the palate before raising it with more spice. It was such a gentle rocking back and forth between the spicy and the soothing; an exploration of the senses rather than an assault. I left uplifted, fully fulfilled but not full, with room to maneuver.*
>
> ◆
>
> *George V. Wright, writer and gardener, Bayside, New York*

away from meat as a regular item of diet and to regard the cow as sacred. As vegetarianism became variously a religious requirement (as among the Jains who revere all life), a philosophy, or simply the normal practice, other aspects of gastronomy also became codified. Most visible is the notion of purity and pollution. Hence, for example, a Brahmin rarely traveled because his food had to be cooked and served only by another freshly bathed Brahmin. He also would not go to a restaurant or other public eating place where food would likely be *jhoota* or unclean, and this is the kind of thing that gave rise to the Indian tradition of entertaining at home only. The best of Indian food is among the best in the world. But it is almost all hidden away in home kitchens. The Indian school runs from the subcontinent northward to Tibet, and westward to Persia. Its influences and offshoots stretch all the way from Southeast Asia to North Africa. Wherever the ancient spice routes have run. Routes which you, the Fearless Diner, can still trace in your travels.

TIPS

➤ Wash your hands, and your mouth, before and after meals.

➤ Eat only with the right hand.

➤ Never offer another diner, not even your spouse, food from your plate.

➤ In some circles, touching a communal dish is taboo. Watch your fellow diners for guidance.

➤ Indians traditionally don't thank their hosts for dinner, as saying "thank you" is a form of payment, which would diminish the host's generosity. You may compliment the chef, but quietly, no effusive praise. To show your gratitude for the meal, return the favor.

➤ The best vegetarian cooking in India is in the city of Madras. The hottest cooking can be found in the state of Andra Pradesh.

➤ All Indians eat with their hands, but they don't all eat the same way. In the north they are rather dainty, and pick up morsels with their fingertips. As you travel south, you see them dig more deeply into their food, until you get to Kerala and Tamil Nadu where they seem to reach in up to their elbows. You can hear your mother's voice saying, "Stop playing with your food!"

➤ On the long haul trains of India, you'll have food service. They have no restaurant car, but a man will come to take your order, which he will telegraph to a station down the way. When the train arrives at that station, you'll be served. At the next station, your tray will be collected and sent back.

➤ In India make it a point to dine in some of the former palaces turned hotels. The food is nearly as good as what you'll find in home kitchens, and it will afford

—— \\\\\//// ——

Not all Hindus are vegetarians, but they still show reverence for life in the rituals of death, as I learned at the village feast where I was called upon to slaughter the goat. Handing me an antique sword the Headman said, "The law of Jhatka requires a single, clean stroke through the neck. And the sword may not touch the ground." Murmuring incantations, two men held the goat over a woven mat so that the body would not touch the ground either. Nervous and eager to do well, I brought the sword down with all my might. The head flew, and I buried the blade three inches into the dirt. The Headman was not pleased.

◆

*Bruce Harmon,
store manager,
Los Gatos, California*

31

you some of that delicious sauce that only faded glory
and lost empire can produce.

GUSTATORY GOALS

➤ Curiously, the world's worst Indian restaurants are in
India. Even more curiously, the best Indian restaurants
are in London, and they do a land office business selling their spicy food to the English who otherwise favor
a very bland diet. I think Tommy imbibes the British
Empire when he eats Indian. The restaurateur imbibes
Tommy's wallet. Be that as it may, Yankee Doodle, be-
take thy bold self to London and eat once a day every
day in a different Indian restaurant. Eschew macaroni.

➤ The docks of the Indian port of Cochin have been the
spice trade's main port of departure since ancient
times. Go and prowl the narrow, twisty lanes. Smell
the air. Step into the *entrepôt* where the world prices
for pepper are set every day. Talk to the merchants,
each of whom will be happy to recommend his
favorite cure or remedy using Indian spice. Cross the
bay and visit the Indian Spice Board (see Resources
section). Then go eat.

➤ In the state of Kerala, visit the temple of the fiery god-
dess *Kodungallure*, whose fearsome temper can only be
appeased with offerings of pepper. A fearless deity she,
with a well-developed palate. Go and worship at her
altar. Then feast on peppery fare.

➤ India is the world's largest producer and consumer of
chile pepper. The market town of Guntur in the state
of Andra Pradesh is in the country's principal chile
growing region, and is home to the world's largest
chile market. Acres and acres of merchants of gusta-

tory fire offer their produce. The air is so thick with chile that you can smell it long before you arrive. The merchants' eyes and noses constantly run due to the heady fumes. Follow your nose to Guntur.

➤ The coast of East Africa has long had much Indian influence. From the spicy city of Mombassa to Zanzibar, the isle of cloves, eat your way along the coast. Travel by land in one direction, sail by Arab dhow in the other. It's cheaply done. And tasty.

➤ Malaysia is one of many hosts to the Indian school, as well as the Chinese. When the two meet there on the Malay peninsula, the delicious result is Nonya cuisine. Travel the Nonya trail from the Thai border to Singapore.

➤ India is the original land of spice, and there you can find any number of cures, potions, and sacred mixtures of spices. The original use of spices was not culinary but mystical. The special properties of spices were believed to be governed by the stars and planets. Pepper was said to belong to the planet Venus, and many love philters were concocted with it, and practitioners of Ayurvedic medicine still make much use of it. See what you can find. Collect your own apothecary.

——— \\\||/// ———

Take and grind all together in a mortar: 1 ounce black pepper, finely ground, 4 pepper leaves or substitute bay leaves, 1 cup raisins, 1 cup honey. The man who rubs his lingham (nether parts) with this mixture will succeed in bringing even a very old woman into the right frame of mind for love.

◆

Kalyanamala, Indian sage

ƐUROPE (THE WEST)

Be a fearless cook!
—*Julia Child*

I CARRY THE EUROPEAN SCHOOL WITH ME wherever I go. Even if it's as little as a bottle of wine or as large as a whole camp kitchen. Comes in handy, as on an expedition into the Baja California wilderness to search for prehistoric cave paintings. First, my companions Matthew and Garret and I got lost in the poorly charted desert. Then our 1959 four-wheel drive paneled jeep broke an axle. Then night fell. And then a paint-blasting, eye-stinging sandstorm blew up. We were 600 miles from the nearest replacement parts, and there was no AAA to call, and no phone to do it with, and no road to stand on the side of and flag down no passing car. Really not our day. There was nothing for it but to sit tight till the tempest abated, hang a storm candle from the ceiling, and to dine, fearlessly. The weather be damned!

I set up a kitchen in a space between me and the rear doors of the jeep. It was about a foot square. My cutting board went on a case of beer, a one burner stove on the floor, box of spices in Matthew's lap and a canvas bag of provisions hung from the wall. While a bottle of Bolinger champagne cooled in an icebox, I borrowed Garret's pocket knife and quickly boned a chicken I had purchased at our last contact with humanity, removed the skin, and cut it into bite-size pieces. I sliced some scallions, thin. The wild wind roared.

By then Garret had the bottle out and was twisting the cork, letting it ease out ever so slowly. A canteen cup and two coffee mugs did good service as crystal flutes. The happy liquid gurgled in the bottle as it tumbled into our cups and frothed over. We drank to the beastly weather, as high velocity sand ate away the top layers of the jeep's paint:

"To the storm!" Garret offered.

"Yes!" I agreed. "To Meteora!"

"The bitch," said Matt.

I lit the little stove, and in a skillet melted unsalted butter. As it foamed, its sweet, dairy smell filled the cabin. Into the pan I put the chicken, sprinkled it with salt and pepper and began to brown it. We all stopped talking for a moment to listen to the sound as it sizzled, that warm, familiar sound of sizzling meat that says, "Here there is succor." To the meat I added the scallions and we savored their pungent fragrance. The swinging light of the storm candle was too dim for me to judge the meat's doneness, so Matt held the flashlight for me. Garret poured more bubbly, carefully, as the stronger gustings of the wind were causing the high-topped vehicle to rock and sway.

When the chicken was thoroughly browned I added tarragon, a can of mushrooms with their liquor, a box of frozen artichoke hearts (they had thawed days before but had kept well on ice), some chicken stock in bouillon form and a good splash of white wine to deglaze the pan. I brought it to a boil, then reduced the flame and let it simmer. The vapors rising from the pan filled the cabin with moist warmth and spread the delicate, yet earthy smells of mushrooms and artichokes and the subtle, sometimes elusive licorice aroma of tarragon. Outside, Meteora was venting her spleen, but the inside of our cabin began to glow.

When the liquid in the pan had fully reduced I added sour cream and a spoonful of Dijon mustard, stirred it well, brought it quickly to the boil once more to finish the sauce, and it was done. I called it Chicken Baja Provençal. From my bag on the wall I drew out a bottle of red Rioja Spanish wine. We poured the wine into our cups and toasted the sailor's toast: "To those at sea; and so, to us."

And so we dined fearlessly upon some of the most

important fundamentals of the Western culinary tradition. Though the flavor battery of the European school varies greatly with the regions of Northern, Eastern, Southern (or Mediterranean), common to them are wine, or vinegar (which is sour wine); a wide range of herbs such as garlic and onion, basil, bay, mustard, tarragon, dill, parsley, all used more heavily in the South and decreasingly as one travels northward; and all manner of animal products: butter, milk, cream, sour cream, cheese, meat stocks, lard and other rendered fats; organ meats, bones, tendons, spinal cords, brains, and horseflesh. Europeans throw away nothing. A Basque chef urged me to order tripe for lunch one day. "It will make you strong," he assured me, as he made the internationally recognized hand signal for sexual intercourse.

The Mediterranean region relies heavily on olive oil, lemon, tomato, sweet pepper. The use of seasonings is restrained compared to China or India, the purpose being to let the natural flavors of foods speak for them-

_____ \\\\|//_ _____

I never realized how good pig fat could be until I spent a year in Hungary. Centuries of Ottoman rule notwithstanding, the Magyars have turned lard into a delicacy. You can get it smoked, spiced, even toasted. It plays the same role as butter and cheese in Western Europe. A popular snack, which I came to enjoy, is a slice of dense rye bread liberally slathered with lard and sprinkled generously with paprika. Mmmm.

◆

Steve Forney, illustrator, Oakland, California

selves. "It should taste of what it is," goes the saying. To which I have countered from time to time with, "But what if the taste you want is of pungent spices?" If it's a Frenchman, I get a shrug, a mutter, and eyes rolled heavenward; if an Italian, I get curses; a Spaniard will chuckle indulgently (I love the

Spaniards); an Englishman has only a theoretical notion of the sense of taste and will not understand the question.

Europe (and its offshoots in the Americas) has long been blessed with an economy of abundance, regular harvests, plenty of fuel. This has given people the opportunity to develop, over many generations, local and regional ways of managing the soil and producing, processing, storing and ameliorating foods so that they become unique to the place, e.g. Parma ham, Normandy butter, Hungarian wine, Cognac, San Francisco sourdough bread. Their qualities cannot be replicated outside their place of origin. More than any other school, then, the European Flavor Battery includes what I call, "the taste of the soil." I can't tell from the taste where a Chinese pig comes from, but I can tell you if it's Spanish. A steamed bun is a steamed bun in the Middle Kingdom, but in Europe bread carries its national identity in all its particulars. And while booze is booze in India, I can tell you if the wine is from Hungary, France or Italy, the whiskey from Scotland, Ireland, or Kentucky. To dine in the European school is to partake of the very character of the local earth.

In the West I have seen virtually every cooking technique in the wide world employed, and a wider range of kitchen equipment used than in the other schools. Sautéing, then deglazing the pan to make a sauce (as I did in the Mexican storm) is among the most recognizable of European kitchen methods. The making of sauces, especially in France, which influences virtually all of Europe, is widely considered to be the height of culinary technique. While there may be literally hundreds of sauces listed in a French recipe book, they are not a hodge-podge. Each one belongs to a "sauce family" and is made from an original "mother sauce." The mother sauces are: Demi-Glace

(Brown), Velouté (White), Emulsion (such as Hollandaise). I could also make a case for Bechamel and some others as mother sauces, but it is arguable (anything whatever to do with French cookery is subject to endless debate), and this is a small book.

The most common staple food of Europe is bread, leavened and baked. Wheat in the South, rye in the North and East. Cultured dairy products are enjoyed everywhere. Though wine is grown mainly in the South and beer produced mainly in the North, both are consumed everywhere, as are distilled spirits, and all three are used in cooking as well. I have found, to both my pleasure and consternation, that the European school uses more alcohol than the other schools combined. In the South the most popular meats are lamb and veal; immediately to the North beef is favored; in the far North people rely more on fish; in the East pork is second in importance only to China. Smoked and cured meats and sausage are ubiquitous. The Southern diet is low in cholesterol and incorporates a great deal of vegetables and fruits. The Northern diet relies more on animal fats and starches, the Eastern even more. Whenever I'm feeling cholesterol and alcohol deprived, I head for Europe. The European school embraces the lands from the Northern Mediterranean to the Arctic, and most of the Western Hemisphere. The Southern and Eastern Mediterranean are influenced by the European school, as well as by the Indian.

TIPS

➤ Take advantage of the regionality of the European/ Western school. Learn what a place is renowned for, and pursue it. Use restaurant guides, chamber of commerce or tourist board brochures, travel and food magazines, and the recommendations of friends to map out your course. Now you have your mission.

Advance! Share it with the people you encounter along the way. Most will cheer you on, give you good advice. And fellow Fearless Diners will desire to hook up with you and your enterprise. Go forth and conquer!

➤ More than any other school, alcoholic beverages are an integral part of the culture. Learn before you go which countries imbibe moderately and which ones enjoy a good booze-up. Then "when in Rome..."

➤ Southern Europeans don't eat breakfast as we know it. Just a roll or toast and coffee. But Northerners really freight up in the a.m. Plan accordingly.

➤ Don't count on all the wines in France to be great, or even good. They sell a lot of stuff that a self-respecting wino wouldn't drink.

> *In Italy, I found that ordering a cappuccino after dinner may cause such a disturbance as to halt the activity of the entire restaurant. A cappuccino, latte, or any milk-based drink is consumed only in the morning. Ordering one after dinner is equivalent to asking for a bowl of cereal for dessert.*
>
> ♦
>
> *Cailín Boyle, writer, San Francisco, California*

➤ Eat a lot of bread while in Europe. You won't find so much so good anywhere else with the possible exception of San Francisco, California.

➤ In the USA you can travel the barbeque trail from coast to coast via the southern route. Or if you want to be perverse, follow the processed cheese trail.

➤ Seek out the best truck stops on any given highway in the Western World. Try Route 66, the Via Appia, or the Pan American Highway.

GUSTATORY GOALS

➤ In Mexico, sip your way through the Tequila region.

➤ As you cross Spain or Greece, consume, and collect, the regional olive oils.

➤ Italy has more regional specialties than any book could hold, but bread is a good start. Or cheese, or wine, or any damn thing you can think of. Italians know how to eat.

➤ Make a special study of the cured meats and white wines as you travel the Rhine river valley.

> *On a NATO exercise in Europe, our troops had a chance to try each others' field rations. After two days, the "rate of exchange" had settled at three British rations for two French. But nobody wanted the American rations. One French NCO denounced them as "murder." At least, that's what it sounded like!*
>
> ◆
>
> *Keith Kellett, writer,*
> *Salisbury, England*

➤ In the "Resources and References" section of this book, find the suppliers of military fare for several countries. When you visit them, eat their soldiers' combat rations. Charge! When you come home, try the American MRE (Meals Ready to Eat). See which ration puts the most fire in your belly, the most gas in your tailpipe.

➤ Using the Michelin Guide, select an area or route somewhere in Europe. Then visit all the one-star restaurants there and determine which one is the best, or otherwise most memorable.

➤ There are hundreds of different cheeses in France. How many can you taste?

➤ Fast food is everywhere now. How will the taste of
  your Big Mac differ between London, or Oslo, and
  home? Are the fries in Moscow as good or better than
  the ones in Paris? Your friends and neighbors will be
  very amused and interested in your report. Remember,
  you are Fearless, not snobbish. Your nose is in your
  food, not in the air.

*I always eat where the locals do—in France, for instance, in the
Restaurants Routiers which are to be found on the main trunk roads and
which cater mainly to lorry drivers. In them you get a three-course meal
with wine which would cost five times as much in any English restaurant.
Sample menu: hors d'oeuvres, main course of rabbit with noodles, or
braised guinea fowl, and duck confit, dessert or cheese, coffee. The wine
will be a rough but perfectly acceptable red vin de pays. You don't need to
speak French—the staff won't speak English, but if you can't understand
French menus, you shouldn't be allowed out on your own anyway.*

◆

Janet MacDonald, writer, Surrey, England

III

MANNERS AND MORES

The world was my oyster, but I used the wrong fork.
—*Oscar Wilde*

WHY IS IT THAT I CAN BELCH freely in one country, but not even put my elbows on the table in another? I've caused embarrassment to my hostess in India by thanking her for the meal; I've upset a fellow diner in Japan by topping off my own beer glass; I've caused Englishmen to go away hungry because I failed to ask the requisite *three* times if they would like more; and I've nearly precipitated a panic because I arrived at a Bedouin dinner in the company of a lady in culottes! And of course I've used my left hand in a culture where such a thing is disgusting. And how is it that I have met someone on the streets of a foreign city and half an hour later he's taking me home to dinner, yet in the neighboring country the people would not think of opening their homes to strangers and would do all their entertaining in restaurants?

Table manners, and the rules of hospitality, do not necessarily make sense. Nor is it their primary function to make sense. Like the etiquette at a formal dance or church service, or the wearing of neckties or wedding bands, their function is to affirm your status as a member of society. And when arriving in a society not your own, they will greatly ease your entry, if you take the time to know them.

Even in those societies whose manners are relatively simple they are just as important, indeed sometimes more important for there being the fewer measures of your "civilized" behavior. Years ago I was dining with a jungle-dwelling tribe in the interior of Borneo. From what I could observe, the only criterion of polite conduct while eating was to speak in a not-too-loud voice. Then I stood up and walked to my backpack to retrieve something, and brought the whole meal to a dead stop. In standing up and walking, rather than crouching and scooting across the floor, I had elevated my head above those of the elders while at dinner. At first quite upset, my gracious hosts recalled that I was an untutored foreigner and so declined to take offense. In earlier years, such a discourteously elevated head would have ended up on a pole.

But even a setting that's a lot closer to home can put egg on your face. The formal English dining room of the E&O Hotel in Penang, Malaysia was empty that evening except for two waiters. All the people were in the lounge. "Must be a thirsty night," I thought, and went into the lounge with the others. The place was really crowded and everybody dressed to the nines, just like I happened to be. A waiter asked me if I wanted

In certain orthodox Hindu households of Nepal or India, you may find yourself being served food outside the kitchen or in the front porch. This simply means that you, a foreigner and thus a non-Hindu, are considered an untouchable, therefore impure. Also, in most Nepali households, meals are eaten silently, especially if you are in a traditional home and eating while sitting on the floor. So do not try to start a conversation. However, it is not only polite, but eminently desirable, to burp—yes, loudly and grandly!—after a meal in a Nepali home. Your burp assures the host that you indeed enjoyed your food. But refrain from farting!

◆

Raj Khadka, editor, Berkeley, California

a drink. "Sure," I said, "gin and tonic." He went away and came back with the drink and before I could pay him he

left. "Okay," I said. "Maybe he's in a hurry. He'll come back."
I milled around and chatted amiably with a few people and
the drink went pretty fast. As I finished it the waiter came
back and asked if I wanted a refill. Again he brought me the
drink and left before I could pay him. That's when I noticed
that nobody was paying. The bartenders were pouring
liquor and beer like it was Kool Aid and nobody was col-
lecting any money.

Then a man in a turban, I guess he was a Sikh, stood up
and hollered, "It's almost the time! Everybody, it's almost the
time!" and everybody perked up and looked eager. "Please
the gentlemen with the golf clubs." And these four guys
with putters lined up shoulder-to-shoulder at the doorway
with their clubs held up at "port arms." Now I happened to
be standing there and so these four guys with raised clubs
are facing me and they look a little more perked up and
eager than the rest of the crowd.

Then the Sikh yelled, "Now the gentlemen with the tennis rackets." So four more guys come over, with tennis rackets at "port arms" and start lining up facing the golfers.
"Would you mind stepping aside, sir?" the Sikh said to me.

I moved over to a place where I'm at least a couple of
club lengths away and looking down the corridor these
eight guys have formed next to the door. "Is this some weird
Asiatic game of lacrosse?" I wondered. "Do they get
liquored up and then go at each other with clubs and rackets? After all, in the supper clubs of Thailand they like to
roll out the mat and do a little kick boxing. Maybe it comes
down from some ancient blood sport, formerly played with
scimitars, but the British made them quit it and use lesser
implements of destruction. I hope it doesn't turn into a wild
scrimmage and I get clobbered in the confusion."

Suddenly the Sikh hollered "Now!" and the eight guys
lifted their weapons up above their shoulders and crossed

them, forming a guard of honor. The band struck up "Happy Birthday" and everybody started singing. In walked the Sultan of Penang! Behind him were who I took to be two of his wives and a teenage daughter.

Remember where I was standing. Looking right down the muzzle of this cannon that was going to shoot the Sultan straight at me! He shook a couple of hands as he came my way, smiling and highly pleased at this display of affection by his people. And there I was,

I have trouble remembering the eat-only-with-the-right-hand rule in India, so I sit on my left hand during the meal.

♦

Margo True, staff editor, Gourmet, *New York*

standing like a schlep with my jaw hanging, the Sultan coming at me, the fool who had just crashed a private party for the biggest bigwig on the whole damned island. And I was only trying to get a good dinner! I started singing Happy Birthday. With feeling. When the Sultan got to me he reached out and shook my hand and said, "Good to see you," and he moved on. "Happy birthday Your Excellency," I sang.

I began to wonder if I might brazen this out and stay for what would surely be a great feast. After all, nobody in the lounge had suspected I was an uninvited guest. I had already had two drinks on His Excellency and was feeling pretty good. I had seen no indication of assigned seating in the dining room. Ah, but what I had seen dashed my plans and sent me out the door. The tables were all set with *Service à la Russe,* the most daunting table practice in all the Great Gastronomical World. I was not prepared. Fearlessness requires preparedness. Let me explain.

It may seem that the world outside the American (or Western) shores is fraught with peril for even the most fearless diner. But I tell you it ain't so. The formal Western table has more opportunities to make a fool of yourself than all the others combined. I find that in most places, if you observe the natives and do as they, you'll be all right most of the time. But at the formal Western table the natives are inscrutable, and cannot be relied upon to guide you through the murky waters of starched napery etiquette. So rely on me. Here is the definitive roadmap for navigating even the most torturous table. Following that you'll find some useful tips and wisdom for the manners and mores, customs, and hospitality of other cultures.

THE TABLE SETTING

The individual place setting you see in the following illustration is the most formal setting you'll ever encounter: *Service à la Russe,* or Russian style. In this style a filled plate is never set in front of a diner, fearless or otherwise. The courses are individually served at the table by a waiter, one

for each diner. Conquer the *Service à la Russe,* and you will be invincible at any table setting in the Western world and wherever the ways of the Western world have been adopted, from Ougadogou to Lhasa. Let's walk through it together.

➤ **The Lay of the Land**

Three forks to the left of the service plate; three knives to the right. The small fourth fork, the oyster fork, the one at the far right of the place setting, with the tines resting in the bowl of the soup spoon.

After the soup spoon, going from outside to inside on both left and right, are the fish fork and knife, followed by the meat fork and knife. Next to the dinner plate, the salad fork and knife. The sherry glass sits above the soup spoon (sherry being served with soup); the white wine glass (for fish) above the fish knife; and the red wine glass (served with meat) above the meat knife. Behind the red wine glass find the water goblet. The champagne flute (or it might be a tulip, but never a coupe) is next to the water goblet. Start from the outside and work your way, course by course, towards the center.

➤ **The First Course**

Use your oyster fork to eat clams, oysters, and shrimp cocktail. Don't cut the shrimp with a knife unless it's served flat on a plate. If in a tall vessel, spear them with your fork and eat them in two or three bites. The lettuce in the dish is for garnish only, not to be eaten.

When you're finished, the waiter will remove the cocktail dish (from the right), and leave your service plate on the table. On that he'll set the soup dish and plate, and then serve the soup (from the left).

➤ **The Soup Course**

Your next utensil on your right is your soup spoon. Take it at the end of the handle, thumb on the top. Lean forward slightly, so as not to spill any food in your lap, and dip the spoon sideways into the soup at the edge nearest you. Just skim the surface, rather than delving deeply, moving the spoon away from you.

Sip from the side of the spoon, and avoid putting the entire spoon in your mouth. And do so with a minimum of noise. If you want to slurp, go to China, and enjoy.

To get the last spoonful, lift the rim of the soup plate slightly to tip the bowl away from you, and continue to spoon the soup from the outer edge of the bowl. Leave the spoon resting on your plate.

At a table of this formality, even the most fearless diner won't try to do two things at the same time. If it's chowder, for example, and it's served with crackers, set the spoon down and take a bite of cracker, then set it down. Don't hold it in one hand, the soup spoon in the other, and alternate between. This makes you look like an eating machine. I'm sorry to say that here you don't break crackers into your soup.

➤ **Bread and Butter Plate**
There are no special plates for bread and butter at this table because they are not served at a formal dinner. However, at less formal affairs, as well as dinner in the finer restaurants, there will likely be a small bread and butter plate at your left. The butter knife should be resting on it.

Always break bread rather than cut it. Butter only a small piece at a time and eat it in one bite. A big ragged hunk of bread slathered with butter and with teethmarks all over it is an unappetizing sight.

➤ The Fish Course

Removing your service plate, the waiter replaces it with a heated plate for the fish course. The fish knife's sword-like shape harkens back to the nineteenth century when it was common to bring the fish to the table whole, head and tail still intact, and perform acts of skillful butchery on it.

To look like you really know what you're doing, hold the knife like you would a pencil, and use the broad side of the blade to gently lift and separate sections of the fish. But if you're served a boneless fillet, you can dispense with it entirely. Leave it on the table and cut the fillet with the side of your fish fork.

➤ Serving Yourself

At the formal banquet, food is removed from your right (remember that "remove" and "right" both begin with R) and served on your left.

Your waiter presents the platter, you take the serving fork in your left hand and the spoon in your right, maneuver a portion onto your plate, and return the serving fork and spoon side by side on the platter.

➤ The Main Course

The dinner knife and fork are the larger utensils and will be used next when the main course, usually meat or poultry, is served.

➤ American vs. European or Continental Style

Americans tend to be "fork-shifters." We hold the fork, tines down, in the left hand, and saw away with the knife in our right hand. Then we set the knife down, shift the empty fork to the right hand, tines up, and spear or scoop the food and carry it to the mouth. Then we shift back and start the whole process over again. Why we go through such a lot of wasted motion, I don't know. The European way is more efficient.

Keep your fork in the left hand, tines down. Cut food with knife held in right hand. Lift food to mouth with left hand. Simple, more elegant (in the mathematical sense), and less distracting. Please try it.

➤ The Code

At formal banquets, and at good restaurants, the staff know by the positions of the knife and fork whether you've merely paused to converse, are waiting for a second helping, or if you're finished eating

If you've just paused to speak or listen, set your utensils in the resting position: fork crossed over the knife, on the plate, tines down.

If you're finished eating, set knife and fork, tines down, parallel to one another, diagonally across the plate.

If you want another helping, position the knife and fork, parallel, along the rim of the plate, at the top. The handles will be at two o'clock, the blade and tines near eleven o'clock.

If for any reason the Code fails, just establish eye contact with the waiter. He'll come ask what you want.

Waiters (and waitresses) prefer not to be addressed as sir, miss, honey, ma'am, etc. "Waiter" (or "Waitress") is the only appropriate form of address. It is an honorable term for one who works a hard and useful job.

➤ Salt and Pepper

Salt and pepper shakers should always be passed, and kept, together, even though tablemates might ask only for one or the other. At some tables you may find the salt in a dish called a salt cellar, rather than in a shaker. The salt cellar usually has a tiny salt spoon, which you can use to place a spoonful of salt at the edge of your plate and dip each forkful of food into. If there's no spoon, you can use the edge of your clean knife, or lift it and gently sprinkle.

Don't ask for hot sauce. If the food is bland, suffer. Eat small portions, then go out for something tasty.

➤ Salad

Despite our modern American custom of serving salad at the beginning of a meal, at a formal table it comes last. The reason is a good one: the vinegar or lemon juice in salad dressing can spoil the taste of the wine served with dinner. Who could argue?

Your salad fork and knife are the small pair closest to your plate. And despite admonitions to the contrary, it's okay to use your knife to cut a lettuce leaf to bite size.

Salad will either be set in front of you as a separate course, or on a plate at your left, above the bread and butter plate, to be taken with the main course. After the salad your waiter will clear the table, remove the salt and pepper shakers, and sweep the crumbs away.

➤ Glassware

Glasses follow the same order as the silverware, moving inward from right to left.

In the illustration, the Y-shaped glass positioned just above the soup spoon is the sherry glass. Again, you often get sherry with soup.

White wine is paired with fish, and its glass is above the fish knife.

Next is the red wine glass, somewhat larger than the white. It generally does more business.

Nearest to the center is your water goblet, largest of all the glasses. I think the original message of its size was that you were to drink more water than wine. Ha!

If champagne is on the menu, you'll recognize its glass by its unmistakable tall, slender shape. Champagne is often poured with dessert.

The sherry glass will be removed after the soup. All of the others remain so you can enjoy them at your leisure throughout the course of the meal.

➤ **Dessert**

When the waiter brings the dessert plate, it may have a finger bowl on it, flanked by the dessert fork and spoon. Place the silver on either side of the plate. Put the bowl on the table, to the upper left of your plate.

At a very, very formal dinner, you may be served three desserts: an ice, a sweet, and fresh fruit. A fresh plate is brought for the fruit, as well as a small fruit knife and fork. You cut and peel most fruits, but you can eat grapes with your fingers.

➤ **Finger Bowls**

Twirl the tips of your fingers into the finger bowl. Dry them on your napkin. It's okay to delicately dab the tips of your moistened fingers to your lips, and then lightly touch your napkin to your lips.

➢ Oops!

If you drop your fork on the floor, ignore it, unless it's a hazard to navigation. If so, discreetly use your foot to move it to a safe place. Then pick up the next utensil in line and sally forth undaunted.

Should you knock over your water goblet, set it right as quickly as possible, throw a napkin over the puddle and carry on.

If you spill water on the person next to you, offer your napkin and apologize, but don't try to pat the person dry yourself. Especially if it's somebody of the opposite sex.

Remember that the waiters and the rest of the staff are there to serve, not to intimidate. It's their job to be alert and to know what to do, quickly and quietly.

TIPS

➢ While a guest in an Arab home, don't admire anything too much. Your host will

---

_\\\\\\//_

At the next village we asked if we could set up camp inside its compound, away from the hyenas and the lions of West Africa. Having obtained permission to camp from the old chief, we gave him a bag of hard candy in place of the customary cola nuts. He didn't seem to know what it was, so I took one out, it was a blue one, wrapped in plastic, and I mimed eating it. "Yum. Good," I said, and handed it to him. Smiling, he popped it into his mouth, plastic and all. He spit it out and looked at us like we'd played a bad trick at his expense. I quickly picked it off the ground and unwrapped it, miming again to put it in his mouth. And the chief, being a chief, had the good grace to try again.

◆

*Carla King, writer,
San Francisco, California*

feel obliged to give it to you.

➤ When in Australia or England, never say, "I'm stuffed." It has a highly sexual connotation.

➤ In England the tea tray is presented to the senior woman at the table. As Mistress of the table, she then serves, and conducts the proceedings. If no other woman is present, the honor goes to the senior gentleman present.

➤ In societies where people eat with their hands, such as India or Arabia, it is a universal practice to eat only with the right hand. Never bring the left hand to your mouth. The left hand is the toilet hand. Under strict Muslim law, a thief is punished by cutting off his right hand. Of course if you cut off his left hand, the right becomes the toilet hand, and the amputee must forever suffer the indignity of eating with his bum-cleaning hand.

➤ Gift giving can be one of the most dangerous mine-fields the Fearless Diner can wander into. Read your country guidebooks closely on this subject.

Do not take a Moroccan's invitation to tea or lunch lightly. These are not eat-and-run affairs, so expect to spend the entire afternoon. Bring a gift. Be prepared to answer personal questions, to take a nap, to not ask about his wife, and to slurp your tea and pretend it's hot. Most importantly: whether it's for eating or for passing, never use your left hand. For traveling vegetarians: tell your host that you would love nothing more at that moment than to eat his eyeball or monkey meat stew, but that "the doctor" simply will not let you.

◆

Brett Allan King,
journalist, Madrid

That said, when you are a guest at dinner, it is never inappropriate to bring your host some inexpensive token of your homeland. I often rely on a package of M&Ms. Plain, not peanut. Some people don't care for nuts, but everyone likes chocolate.

➤ Where chopsticks are used, don't spear the food with them. And don't stick them into a bowl of food and leave them there. That is a funerary practice.

➤ Some countries where hospitality is practiced in the home:

Belarus	Israel
Columbia	Jordan
Denmark	Kuwait
Equador	Mexico
Egypt	New Zealand
Greece	Philippines
Guatemala	Sri Lanka
India	

➤ Some countries where hospitality is practiced in restaurants:

Chile	Paraguay
China	Poland
Finland	Spain
France	Taiwan
Italy	Thailand
Japan	Turkey
Malaysia	Uruguay
Netherlands	

➤ Some countries where home hospitality is a special honor:

Argentina
Australia
Belgium
Czech Republic
England

Germany
Korea
Russia
Venezuela

➤ Carry plenty of your
business cards. People
love to receive them. In
some countries they col-
lect them like baseball
cards. If you don't have
any, make some up.
Even if they identify you
as nothing grander than
a "Sanitation Engineer."

> _____ \\\\\\// _____
>
> *In Ethiopia, the eating tool of
> choice is the hand, and often
> not your own hand, either. It
> was there I encountered the rit-
> ual of feeding others. It's called
> gursha and is a revered and
> honored practice where the
> feeder dips spongy bread in a
> common platter of saucy veg-
> etables and then places the roll
> into the mouth of the eater.
> Gursha expresses respect and
> caring and to refuse it is
> unthinkably disrespectful.*
>
> ◆
>
> *Sara Hare, journalist,
> Oakland, California*

GUSTATORY
GOALS

➤ When you have mas-
tered *Service à la Russe*,
save up a pocketful of
money and dine in one
of the Western World's temples to gastronomy.
Consult your guidebook to avoid places frequented
by the ultra-rich, or the oh-so-hip, or anybody from
Hollywood.

➤ Travel to a place where people enjoy feasting outdoors,
e.g. Polynesia, Africa, Argentina. With due attention to
the local etiquette and proper form, give a great feast.
Entertain, even astonish, your guests by singing a local

traditional song. It can be done without too great expense, and you will be remembered fondly for years.

➤ Stay in a private home. Shopping and cooking and dining with your hosts is one of the best ways to see the world through cuisine. There are many Home Stay agencies that can hook you up with the kind of people you'll like. See the Resources and References chapter.

➤ Offer to bring from the market to the kitchen of your new friend or host all the makings of a fine feast common to your hometown or state. Prepare the meal yourself, and serve it, and entertain your "guests" just as you would do at home. Your diners will be moved by your generosity, and intrigued to see another people's traditions, manners, and mores at such an intimate level, and without even having to leave home. Some suggested menus:

For serving diners of the Chinese school, remember that they usually avoid raw vegetables and dairy products, so salads and cheese are out. Try hamburgers and french fries, or spaghetti with a tomato-based sauce, and apple pie for dessert. For a spicier feast serve chile con carne or gumbo or barbeque, with corn bread and fried greens or okra. Follow with a sweet potato pie to make them swoon. If you want to get really elaborate, give a Thanksgiving dinner.

In the Indian school, you would do well with fried chicken, gravy, and biscuits with peas or spinach. Buy some goat meat and offer them grilled "lambchops" with mint chutney, roasted potatoes, and braised vegetables. If you can acquire maple syrup, serve pancakes and eggs.

In Europe, USA is synonymous with New York steak. You'll have to go to the butcher and have it cut special for you, as it's generally not available outside the Americas. You will find it pricey. But at the end of your days (not to mention the end of your trip) you will regret your economies more than your extravagances. Go for it. NOTE: Do not try this idea in a Brahmin or kosher kitchen. Too many land mines.

Discovering Bali's culture through the medium of cuisine is as easy as going home. A Balinese home-stay, that is. Your host family will be delighted if you participate in preparing the day's meals. Be ready: it takes a lot of time and elbow grease to slice, dice, and finely chop all the ingredients. The women spend a great deal of time preparing food offerings for the temple. You can sit with them and watch or help as they mold food into special shapes, construct it into towers, balance it on their heads, and gracefully carry it to the altar. Among the Balinese in the kitchen, inclusion of the stranger is as natural as their smiles.

◆

Gina Comaich, teacher, Oakland, California

IV
ℛ E S T A U R A N T 𝒮 U R V I V A L

Well if it looks just like chicken, and it tastes just like chicken,
why don't they just give me the Goddamn chicken?

—Bobcat Golthwaite, In Performance

———

RAPTLY I LOOKED THROUGH THE WINDOW of the elegant restaurant on the rue St. Germain in Paris. Smartly dressed and perfectly coiffed ladies of fashion sat with pinstriped men who drank champagne from Baccarat crystal. They ate snails and Steak Tartare, and eyed each other hungrily. The tables were set with *Service à la Russe.* "I ain't afraid of you," I thought. "I know the drill now. I can do this as well as any of you high-toned airheads. The Sultan's birthday is history!" Turning to my companion I said, "Let's eat," and led her inside.

I put on no airs. I spoke to no one down my nose. (My nose was too busy appreciating the smells emanating from the kitchen.) Having acquired it the day before, I already knew the menu, and had studied it well. I ordered with casual confidence for the two of us. So far, the waiter seemed to have recognized a kindred spirit in me, and was even willing to speak English, a thing almost unheard of among Parisian waiters, though many of them *know* how to speak English. Then came the wine list. It was not the one I had seen the day before! I recognized nothing on it. The Sommelier was off somewhere. I faked it. I ordered three different wines and I hit the jackpot. A buzz went through the restaurant that, according to my companion, who spoke some French, the American gentleman at table #3 really knew his onions. To this day I don't know what I ordered, but it was good. And the chef came out to congratulate *me*! He was very gratified that he was attracting patrons of such careful taste. Some days, if you've prepared yourself, you just can't lose.

A lifetime of dining on the road has taught me that the three schools of cuisine each have their own school of restaurant. The Chinese restaurant school is the oldest. (In fact the oldest restaurant in the world today is Ma Yu Ching's Bucket Chicken House in Kaifeng, China, operating continuously for over 900 years. Now under new management, so I am told.) The Chinese restaurant's origins are with the sidewalk hawker and food stall operator, catering mainly to townsfolk and travelers from all stations in life. It is a place where people gather to dine in community and be restored. Given its unpretentious origin and purpose, it's pretty "user friendly." I've made fewer social gaffes in Chinese eateries than any other. As long as you know your chopsticks and don't act like an ass, you'll get by very easily in any good Chinese restaurant.

The Indian restaurant descends from the inn, or the *caravansari*. Its purpose was to feed travelers who would likely not be back again to complain. Modern Indian restaurants, and those outside India, are

> *Our favorite restaurant tactic in China is to find a place full of locals and no English menu. Then we look casually around to see what people are eating and, if something looks interesting, point it out to the waiter. If nothing strikes our fancy, we just smile a lot and walk into the kitchen. Everything we could want is there. We then simply point to ingredients, and make cutting and cooking motions to indicate how we want it done. Works every time. Just smile a lot.*
>
> ◆
>
> *Paul Harmon, championship dancer, San Jose, California*

usually European-style restaurants that happen to serve Indian food.

The European restaurant (as opposed to the inn), a place where fine food and wine are enjoyed in a civilized and civilizing atmosphere, first became customary in France shortly after the French Revolution. Up until that time the rich ate fancy fare and the poor ate porridge. As the French nobility dissolved, two never-before-seen phenomena appeared: an emerging middle class with a bit of money to spend, and a lot of talented chefs made unemployed by the decapitation of their masters. The entrepreneurial among the chefs opened their kitchens and, in the spirit of *egalité,* proclaimed that anyone with the price of a meal could enjoy the same food, service and ambiance as the late king and his court. Thus, from the king's own table, this splendid institution comes to us.

Because of this royal lineage, it can also be fraught with snobbery, high cost, prissyness, and an overweening sense of punctilio. Or so it can sometimes seem. But travel in the Western World would be severely diminished without visiting some of its great restaurants, so don't be intimidated. A little knowledge and preparation will steer you around the pitfalls and ensure you a good journey and a good dinner.

The most important things to remember in European-style restaurants (indeed any restaurant) are: why you are there and who is paying the freight. When I step into a fine restaurant I know I'm going to pay a lot, so I expect to get a lot. And I expect the staff to remember that it is I who pay their salaries. I am not there to see or be seen, engage in silly games of one-upmanship, or to be spoken to as anything less than a most welcome visitor. I am there for a great gastronomic experience. If I don't think I'm going to get it, I leave. So should you. There's not a restaurant on the face of the globe that's worth a bellyache, whether bacterial or emotional. Being a Fearless Diner, you should not fear to leave an establishment where you know you won't enjoy yourself.

That said, don't go in with a chip on your shoulder. Most successful restaurants are all they should be. The staff work at a very tough and demanding job, and should be given the same respect that you want from them. Look for the good and praise it, tip accordingly, and take home a copy of the menu as a souvenir.

Parisian waiters are notorious for ignoring foreign customers. The waiters at an expensive restaurant were taking their time waiting on me during a recent trip. I stood up and threatened to leave. The waiter scurried over and I demanded to know why they were taking so long. Service improved immediately. Later, my fish was served partly frozen. I had the serving sent back to the chef and an entirely new plate was quickly produced. Lesson: the French respect those who stand up for their rights.

◆

Sean O'Reilly, writer and editor, Glendale, Arizona

TIPS

➤ Before you go, get good, up-to-date advice about the restaurants on your route. A restaurant guidebook is handy, but they can be very out of date as the restaurant business is "fluid." Get the latest edition.

➤ Study the local cuisine before your journey so that you can discuss your dinner intelligently when ordering. Waiters appreciate the serious diner, and will take pains to see you well served.

➤ Just in town and don't know where to go for a really fine dinner? Ask the hotel desk or a taxi driver, "Where would you go if you wanted to propose marriage?"

- Make reservations, even if only an hour ahead. If you don't speak the language, your hotel can do it for you.

- Be punctual. A busy establishment can only hold a table for 15–30 minutes. If you're going to be late, or not show, call.

- If possible, get the menu in advance and study it. If you've never done this, you may well be amazed at what this simple activity can do for your dining experience.

- On the menu, disregard anything you can get elsewhere or from a can: caviar, paté, steak or roast beef, ice cream (unless they make their own). What remains are the classics and the restaurant's signature dishes. These are why you're here.

- Be aware that nowadays most hors d'oeuvres either come from a can,

---

In the city of Ghent in Belgium I walked into a restaurant looking for what I had craved so long: real Belgian waffles. Not the bastardized American version, but the real McCoy. I ordered. And as if E.F. Hutton had spoken, the place fell silent. "We certainly would not have them at this time of day, Monsieur." Turns out the Belgians just eat them like toast, or as a side dish at dinner. Merde!

♦

Eugene Robinson, technical editor, East Palo Alto, California

---

I went to a restaurant in Agadir, Morocco. The menu read like this: Beef Tongue, Foot, Tail, Stomach, and so on, listing body parts, as opposed to preparation. I decided to order the foot because the tail was too close to the bum. I was quite surprised by what I got. The dish tasted delicious: braised beef shanks.

♦

Julia Shanks, writer, United Kingdom

or are scaled down versions of entrees without accordingly scaled down prices. They won't show the kitchen's talent, but they will improve its profit margin. Soup will often be a better gauge of culinary character, and cost less.

➤ Remember that "today's special" may in fact be today's "hard-sell" item. They gotta move it or lose it.

➤ Truly great wines should be paired with very simple foods, otherwise they distract from each other. Avoid their only-the-Sultan-of-Brunei-can-afford-them prices in restaurants. Buy them at a wine shop (or a discount store if you can) and enjoy them in your hotel with cheese, oysters, or Steak Tartare.

➤ In all the theatrical folderol that goes with serving wine, only two things matter:
1. Be sure the bottle is opened in your presence, after you have approved the label. Otherwise, send it back.

—— ⚜ ——

There is nothing like the smell of a trattoria in Rome. Italian restaurants elsewhere have as much relation to a Roman trattoria as pornography has to great sex. In Rome when the door to a trattoria is opened, in one grand sniff the meal is revealed in the small mosaic of its parts, similar to the way an overture gives you a musical sample of what is to come.

Prosciutto, salami, garlic, onions, oregano, wine, coffee, bread, olive oil, fresh white linen, vinegar, vigorous noise and convivial clatter, stone, dampness, marble, and almonds chorale into libidinousness which is stopped, (but no one realizes it) by the formality of the place and the starch and snap of the waiters.

◆

George V. Wright, writer and gardener, Bayside, New York

---

2. The purpose of that little taste test is simply to determine if the wine has spoiled in transit or storage. Nowadays, that is exceedingly rare. Of the countless bottles of wine I've taste tested I've sent back only one. It had been stored upright near the stove and was cooked to medium-well. I had a beer with that dinner. And I never went there again.

➤ Do not hesitate to ask the waiter to explain the bill if you think it's in error.

———— \\\//// ————

Oftentimes when we travel we'd love to sample the fare of a famous restaurant, but with the tariff for a single dinner akin to that of our airfare to the place, the idea isn't practical. Lunch, of course, is a less pricey alternative. But how about breakfast? Especially if the eatery is connected with a hostelry of some sort, they will offer breakfast in the same room, with the same ambiance, the same service, and the same quality of food as diners enjoy for an evening meal.

◆

Judy Wade, travel writer,
Phoenix, Arizona

➤ Do not pay for anything you did not order. If something you didn't order is brought to your table, it may or may *not* be gratis. Find out, and say "thanks" or "no thanks" accordingly.

➤ Tipping is *not* a universal custom. Consult your guidebook, then if called for, tip by the local scale, usually 10-15% of the total, not including tax. Do *not* tip if a service charge is on the bill. If you are served by a captain or head waiter in addition to the waiter, they get about 5%.

➤ If for some unfortunate reason, food or service is unsatisfactory and you can get no satisfaction, get up and leave. But stop on the way out and politely (shouting is counter-productive) but firmly tell the manager or maitre d'hotel. If that august person is worth his or her salt, he/she will make it better, or invite you to return as a guest of the house. Failing that, write to the proprietor and the author of your restaurant guidebook. I have written a few such epistles, and I have found that if I can lead with praise, close with praise, and sandwich my complaint in the middle, I'll virtually always get good results. Only once in my life has this approach failed me. And if you want to know what and where that guilty establishment is, write to me and I'll tell you! And they know who they are!

> _____ ⚘ _____
>
> *Avoid eating meat (especially messed-about meat products like sausages) or other potentially infected foods which have been kept lukewarm on buffets in big hotels in hot countries. The superficial veneer of westernisation in tourist resorts like in Thailand can lead you into a false sense of security. You think that the precautions will be maintained and then if you do get sick there will be adequate competent medical resources to treat you. Travellers need to remember things are different in Asia*
>
> ◆
>
> *Dr. Jane Wilson-Howarth, physician, Nepal*

➤ The internationally recognized gesture for "Check, please" is to make a writing motion across the palm of your hand. In Europe and much of Asia you must do this, or call for it, otherwise it will be assumed you are not ready for it.

➤ Flies are ubiquitous in much of the non-industrial world, and can be especially vexing at tables of open-air restaurants. They are drawn largely to residues on the table. Carry a bandanna or large hankie which you can moisten from your water bottle and then use to clean the table. It also works well as a fly whisk, and as the napkin they never give you.

➤ In East Asia many restaurants use non-disposable wooden chopsticks. These are hard to keep clean and can give you a bellyache. Carry your own plastic or metal chopsticks, and use them. No one will take offense.

➤ Perhaps the most survivable, "user friendly" restaurant in the world is the No Hands Restaurant in Bangkok, Thailand. As the name implies, you are so well taken care of that you won't even have to lift a finger. Whether you are male or female, an attractive young woman will be assigned as your dinner companion, and she will not only keep you company, advise you about the menu, and pour your drinks, she will feed you with her own hands. You only have to sign the check.

> In Lebanon, don't pass up a chance for a mezze. This eating extravaganza can include up to 40 different dishes. As you run out of room at your table, and the latest additions get piled on glasses and other plates, you realize that in Lebanon, eating is a national sport. And the mezze is its World Series.
>
> ◆
>
> Cailin Boyle, writer, San Francisco, California

➤ In many countries, especially in parts of the Islamic world, it is unusual, provocative, scandalous (choose your own adjective, you know what I mean), for a woman to dine alone in a restaurant. You can often mitigate the effect by simply wearing a head scarf. If you still get untoward attention, take out your traveler's sewing kit and sew something. Or pretend to sew something, anything. You will create a powerful image of domesticity that a pious Muslim, home and family being the center of his life, would never molest.

➤ Be aware of local concepts of time. What constitutes unacceptably slow service at home may be the norm elsewhere, especially in tropical countries.

➤ If you can't recognize what you're eating, wait until you finish before asking what it was. You'll enjoy it more.

➤ Using your guidebook, take the time to memorize a few culinary terms. It will greatly facilitate your getting what you like and will help to prevent surprises, like inadvertently ordering organ meats.

> _____ ⋈⋈⋙ _____
>
> *When traveling in Southern China, keep an eye out for an item translated on menus as super deer. You may think this moniker refers to a premium grade of venison, but actually refers to a plate of rat.*
>
> ◆
>
> *Mark Cannon, television writer, Los Angeles, California*

GUSTATORY GOALS

➤ Get in good with a local chef. Such a person can show you people, places, and experiences that you would never know otherwise.

➤ Go on a cooking vacation. There are many restaurants and cooking schools and tour operators that cater to the wandering gastronome desirous of more culinary education. See the Resources section.

➤ Ten good questions to ask the chef:
What is your most unusual cooking experience?
What is your worst cooking experience?
What's good today?
How do you like to use spices?
What is your most important tool in the kitchen?
What were you before?
What is your culinary fantasy, what would you cook, how would it be served and eaten? By whom?
Do women cook for you? (If cook is a single man)
Do men expect you to cook for them? (If cook is a single woman)
What would you not wish to cook?

➤ Keep a gustatory journal of where you ate, what you saw, what you learned. Fill it with recipes, menus, and wine labels you have collected. (Make sure you are not charged for a recipe if you ask for it.) Add sketches of waiters and cooks (if you can draw) and what you talked about or overheard at the table.

The maitre d' fixes you with an intense gaze, and with a sweep of his hand grants permission to leave his exquisite, perfect restaurant. He says only "Bonsoir, monsieur," but his words—so deep, rich (yes, mellifluous)—are a gift, a magnanimous act. You strive to reciprocate, but it comes out too high, absurd: "Bone-swahr," a German dog biscuit which goes skittering across the floor to clatter at the feet of frowning diners. Alas, you are a caveman. You may as well go now to the coat check and ask for your skins and your club and shamble into the night.

◆

James O'Reilly, "Troglodytes in Gaul," Travelers' Tales France

V

$\mathscr{M}$EAT, $\mathscr{F}$ISH
AND $\mathscr{F}$OWL

Every moving thing shall be meat for you.

—*Genesis 9:3*

———

ALL AROUND THE PYRAMIDS of Giza lie villages that have been occupied by Bedouin families since time out of mind. One of them is the family of Amdi Nasr el Nahes. They have been camel and horse breeders for generations. I met Amdi in a coffee house in Cairo where he had come on some family business. I invited him to share coffee and a hookah pipe with me and we became friends in a day. Two days later in the family village, I was adopted. It's amazing, Fearless One, what some coffee, a pipe, and a little hospitality can do in the right place. Amdi and his brother Ali took me trekking across the desert with their camels. "How many years has your family lived here?" I asked Amdi as we packed our gear. He looked at his brother, they both shook their heads.

"I don't know," he said.

"Approximately," I pressed him.

"I don't know, Brother. Since Pharaoh time. How many years is that?"

The morning of our first day out across the Egyptian desert, Amdi and Ali saddled a camel for me whom I had named "Clyde." My friends thought the name hilarious and laughed every time I uttered it. When Clyde was ready to be mounted Ali said, "Now we must teach you how to ride."

"No problem," I said. "I learned how to ride a camel in India. I'll show you." I mounted the seated beast and braced myself for the sudden rise of his hind legs, which maneuver can tumble an unprepared rider head over heels. "*Khush,* Clyde," I said, speaking what I thought was pretty good Camel. "*Khush!*" (Which means "Get up, you lazy camel!") "*Khush,* Clyde!"

Clyde suddenly raised his two left legs, rolled over onto his right side and spilled me on the ground with a "whump." Clyde laughed his camel laugh. It was a sound I would come to know well. Though I had crossed the Great Indian Desert on camelback, and thought myself quite the camelteer, Clyde was out to teach me otherwise. Later on he took to nipping at me with his teeth, as though he would rip out a piece of flesh and eat it in front of me. Miserable beast.

"Clyde is very bad sometimes," Amdi said. "I think we will get rid of him soon." It couldn't have been soon enough for me.

And the camels…eat thereof and feed the beggar and the suppliant.

◆

Koran 22:36

When we returned from the long trek I thought I would never be able to sit down again for the saddle sores Clyde had given me. I also checked repeatedly for broken bones. I was about to depart Egypt in a very sorry state. My spirits soared, though, when Amdi and Ali told they would give me a great feast of farewell in their village. They even said I could bring along some friends I had met earlier in Cairo. "That's great!" I said. "And what's on the menu?"

It was Clyde.

Oh yes, Fearless One. It was Clyde.

Apparently my expression, that of having stumbled upon El Dorado, didn't mean quite the same in Arabic, and

Ali hastened to assure me that, "We eat camel often. Yes. You will find it delicious. Especially camel's foot stew! It will make you very strong."

"It will?" said I, dreamily.

"You will see. The camel butcher is our cousin and he will be at the feast. He eats camel's foot stew every day. And he has three wives and nine children. Yes, it will make you very strong."

"Can we roast him?"

The whole village turned out, and it was said to be the most magnificent feast that anyone had ever attended. Amdi's mother supervised the preparation, and sent Clyde to us in many guises: roasted, stewed, grilled, braised with vegetables, made into soup. I stood by with a notebook, as Mother directed her daughters and daughters-in-law, writing down the recipes. And the anticipation! It was as savory as the meat itself. The Ultimate Cookout was happening before me, in the shadow of

—— \\\||// ——

Then in the distance, I spotted chickens; beautiful, spinning chickens.... They were perfect, naturally plump. Foods are always more wholesome in areas without high-tech agriculture and the attendant short-cuts...bright yellow from herbs, the skin as unblemished as a fine Cuban cigar.... The flesh was meltingly tender; none of that wet sawdusty graininess in the white meat you find in American chickens.

◆

Jim Leff, New York,
in "Morocco Blue"
from Travelers' Tales Food:
A Taste of the Road

the Sphinx, and in my honor no less. And every bruise, indignity, saddle sore, and near-miss with his teeth would fade with every morsel of Clyde. Ah, Clyde, Clyde. I bear you no malice anymore. You were a bad camel, Clyde. But in the end, you were oh so good. Though I never did get a coat of you.

The Fearless Diner desiring meat does well to know what the local geography and culture produce best. Some things are obvious, of course: camels do well in a desert environment, beef cattle don't; goats fare poorly in Siberia. But I have found that culture plays just as important a role in what's good to eat. Cattle can thrive in China, but pork is the premier meat in the Middle Kingdom. And as anyone who has been to India knows, cattle proliferate there but good luck getting a hamburger. (I have had a lamb burger in New Delhi, and it wasn't bad.) I always do some research on my planned destinations, even if I've been there a score of times. I want to know the lay of the land, the price of goods, and what's good to price. My research materials include cookery books, to give me an idea of what pre-dominates at the table.

In deciding how I want my meat prepared, I remember that dry cooking techniques (roasting, broiling, sautéing) work best with the more tender cuts—those portions that are least stressed in ordinary movement. They come main-ly from the back of the carcass from the point between the shoulders to the tail. Tougher cuts should be cooked with moist or wet heat (stewing, braising, pot roasting). In restaurants throughout much of the non-industrial world the carcass is hanging up somewhere in the kitchen, often with skin and head intact, and I can go select the cut I desire. I long ago got used to looking the dead creature in the face and saying, "Hack me off a hunk here."

Of all the items found in a restaurant, the most perish-able is fish. And fish gone bad is one bad bellyache. As a general rule, I head for a popular restaurant at the water's edge in a fishing port as the best assurance of impeccably fresh fish. But even here a note of caution: if the menu lists every fish imaginable, especially those not from local waters, there is no way the kitchen can keep them edible short of freezing. And if frozen fish is okay with you, you can get it a lot cheaper at home. If you have a chance to see your fish before preparation, or you are buying it yourself, check to see that its eyes aren't sunken or opaque, that the gills are ruddy, and the scales intact and adhering to the skin, not flaking off.

Why is it that anything unfamiliar tastes like chicken? Perhaps it's because industrially-produced chickens in the USA and other "developed" countries are so bland that we can compare them to almost anything without too much contradiction. In most other countries of the world chickens are produced in barnyards where they grow up fat, happy, and tasty. I find them almost a universal culinary constant and with a few exceptions (such as India) can usually be relied on. I've bought them live and cut their heads off with a Swiss army knife, then roasted them over a small fire in Mexico, Thailand, Laos, and Kenya, and they yielded me a better dinner at one-tenth the price of a touristy restaurant. And since I shared with others, those barnyard chickens have brought me friends as well as a full stomach.

MEAT

➤ Nobody knows lamb better than a Greek, so seek it out in the land of Homer.

Riding the bus on a two-day trip between Vientiane and Pak Se in Laos is dirty, dusty work, but the food stalls they stop at are great. At one I had a whole rice rabbit, barbequed on a stick. Delicious. Yeah, yeah, I know. It was really a rat. But hey, it tasted like rabbit. Or was it chicken?

♦

Bruce Harmon, store manager, Los Gatos, California

➤ Nobody knows veal better than an Italian. Eat it from the top to the toe, of Italy, that is.

➤ Beef belongs to the Americans and the Argentines. You will rarely go wrong with steaks and roasts in the USA or the pampas.

➤ With the exception of the odd Mexican or Hungarian, only a Chinese chef knows how to get the best out of pork. It is the premier meat in China, so highly regarded that Mao Zedong himself once vowed that every family in China would one day own a pig.

➤ In India they serve what they call "mutton," though we would call it "lamb." In reality, it's goat. And it can be quite good. It can also have the texture of a tire. You pay your money and you take your chances.

> ———— 〰 ————
>
> *In the town of Nijmegen, Netherlands I found a no name place that feeds carnivores. Its house specialty is Fleisch mit Fleisch. In English: "Meat with Meat." No veggies, no potato, no sauce. Just meat. Reindeer, lamb, chicken, beef, pork, and blood sausage. About three pounds of flesh. (Merchant of Venice, take note.) I walked out afterward in a post-prandial/ orgasmic after-glow, a thin sheen of blood from the sausage coating my teeth, content.*
>
> ◆
>
> *Eugene Robinson, technical editor, East Palo Alto, California*

➤ Steak Tartare or Carpaccio? While there is no such thing as a true aphrodisiac, the sight of one's partner consuming raw beef can be pretty close.

➤ Jonesing for a steak in India? Get thyself to Goa, on the Southwest coast. This former Portuguese enclave (until 1961) is still predominately Catholic and carnivorous. You can even get pork chops.

➤ The crust of Beef Wellington is not intended for eating. It's there to keep the meat moist and aromatic during cooking. Remove it to the side of your plate.

➤ "Surf & Turf" is a terrible thing to do to a good piece of meat. Make up your mind: surf *or* turf.

➤ Introduce yourself to hunters. There is hardly a hunter on the planet who doesn't like to eat what he kills. He might have some of his last kill at home and you can bet he's dying to tell you how he got it. He might invite you home to dinner, or out for a weekend's shooting. You can find hunting clubs in the phone book, through tourism brochures, and in the hunting and shooting magazines on any newsstand.

FISH

➤ In Western restaurants, the less tarted up it is, the better. So avoid gloppy sauces and let the natural flavors shine through. Chinese chefs, on the other hand, may be given free rein. Your average Indian cook doesn't know what to do with fish.

➤ Know the source. Was it shipped "fresh" from Maine after first being shipped frozen from France? Does it come from that nearby body of water that is also a conduit for effluent? Ideally it comes from that live tank in front of the restaurant.

➤ Go fishin'. If you have a collapsible rod and small reel, and you know you'll be near water, take your tackle with you. Even if you don't catch anything, you'll likely meet others who have gone fishin', and you can swap tales over beer.

➤ Spectacularly large shellfish are also spectacularly tough and stringy. They are best at early adulthood.

➤ Any seafood emitting odors should be shunned, sent back, not paid for.

> ——— \\\\\\/// ———
> *If I can't see water, I don't order fish.*
>
> ◆
>
> *Jenise Stone, wine collector, Huntington Beach, California*

➤ Fish (when served whole): Slit the fish from gill to tail, just above the middle of its side. Fold back the skin and, with knife and fork, remove bite-size portions of the meat. This will reveal the backbone. Insert the knife under one end of the backbone, and gently lift it our with your fork. Set the bone on the side of the plate. Eat the remaining meat with a fork. Remove any bones from your mouth with your thumb and forefinger.

➤ Lobster: Unless lobster is served out of the shell, as in a salad or as lobster Thermidor, this is a food that you should not order in a formal situation. Your concentration goes to cracking the shell, extracting the meat, and trying not to squirt the juice on the person seated opposite you.

➤ Mussels: Pick them up by the shell and spear the mussel with an oyster fork, or replace the fork with an empty mussel shell, using it as a scoop to extract each mussel from its shell.

➤ Oysters (served on the half shell): Steady the shell on the plate with one hand, and with the other hand use an oyster fork to lift out the oyster, which you then put into your mouth whole. It's okay to pick up the shell and drink the juice after you've eaten the oyster. Oysters in a stew are eaten with a spoon. Fried oysters are eaten with a knife and fork.

➤ Clams: Eat clams in one bite. Use an oyster fork to pick up the clam. You may then pick up the shell and drink the remaining clam juice. Steamed clams: Open the shell and with your fingers pull away the black outer skin covering the neck. Holding on to the neck, dip the clam into the accompanying broth or melted butter, and eat it in one mouthful.

> *Drive-in movie snack bar. Hawaii. Men in Black the feature. "Try this," I said to my wife as I handed her the neatly formed dollop of rice that, with its belt of dried seaweed, looked just like any other piece of sushi. "It's good," she said, taking a bite. "What is it?" My wife had just sampled her first Mr. Musubi—her first piece of Spam sushi. Ah, Men in Black, a drive-in theater, and Spam sushi. Now that was a thoroughly American gastro-travel experience.*
>
> ◆
>
> *Robert Strauss, writer, San Francisco, California*

FOWL

➤ Roast chicken, perfectly done, is one of the best indicators of a skillful pair of hands in the kitchen.

➤ Any dish called "Breast of Chicken *fill-in-the-blank,*" no matter how prepared or denominated, will tend to have all the flavor of cotton.

➤ In India the chicken meets the ax just before it succumbs to starvation. Or so it seems. Chickens in the USA are made of meat and meat by-products. Or so it seems. But in the Middle East raising chickens is nearly an art form.

➤ The ducks in Southeast Asia are some of the best. Try it curried in Thailand or Laos.

➤ Chicken Kiev (or anything stuffed, breaded, and deep fried, for that matter) most likely came to the restaurant in a package from a commercial provider already assembled and frozen, ready to be dropped into the oil. You might as well dine at Denny's.

> _Peking Duck became famous because the Mongolian emperors would insist on their barbecued foods wherever they went. During the 19th century, the emperors would have foreign missionary/journalist groupies on their walkabouts who sent back reports of "the emperor's favorite dish." Such was the romanticism of what is basically a duck-skin sandwich._
>
> ◆
>
> Harry Rolnick, editor, Budapest

➤ Chicken: Unless you're at a picnic or barbecue, chicken is not a finger food. Always use your knife and fork.

➤ Because Peking Duck takes so much time to prepare, give a Chinese restaurant advance notice if you want to order it.

ODDMENTS

➤ In the European or Western school, visit a candy factory. Confectionery is a highly developed art in this school, particularly in Europe. Almost all factories offer tours, and you'll find a people's sweet tooth a useful window on its culture.

➤ No Asiatic cuisine practices the art of confectionery. There is no pastry chef in the kitchen. The perfect meal in the Chinese school is so balanced that sweets are unnecessary. The best thing to follow with is fresh fruit.

➤ Salads (simple bunches of green leaves, oil, and vinegar) come at the end of the meal in Europe, their purpose being to scour the palate after a heavy meal of meats and sauces. They virtually do not exist in China or India, nor do they need to.

➤ Cheese needs to be served at room temperature in order for its subtleties to be available to the senses. Most Europeans know this. When dining in America and you want cheese at the end of your meal, say so upon arrival at the restaurant so they can take it out of the cooler. Don't look for cheese in most of Asia. All you will find is packets of Laughing Cow processed cheese food. The best cultured milk product to be found is yogurt, often made from buffalo milk, and quite good.

➤ Escargots: Served with a special pair of tongs and a double-pronged fork. Grip the snail shell in the tongs, and pick out the snail with the fork. If there's bread at the table, it's perfectly correct—and delicious—to dip the bread into the garlic sauce after you've eaten the snails.

GUSTATORY GOALS

➤ In Nairobi, Kenya, dine at *The Carnivore* restaurant. From the Great Grilling Operation in the center of the main dining room you can select zebra steak, crocodile stew, hippo sausage, and just about anything on four legs that lives in Africa.

➤ You don't have to wait until you're in New England for a clam bake. Any place where the ocean meets the shore and a fish market is nearby will do. If you're on a Greek island, a Mexican bay, a Vietnamese cove, you can dig a hole, line it with rocks, build a fire and throw in the day's catch. It's a wonderful excuse for a party, a great way to make new friends as you all contribute, a large way to repay your hosts, or entertain your guests. The *Joy of Cooking* will tell you how to do it.

➤ Too far from the sea for a clambake? Roast a whole ostrich, or an emu, on a spit. They are available commercially in the Southwest USA, Australia, and Southern Africa. For a smaller party, gather half a dozen friends and one ostrich egg for an omelet fest.

———— ⋙⋘ ————

My family's story of the Steak and Dye Incident reinforced for me at an early age the value of the serendipitous and unexpected in dining. My parents were preparing a steak at my grandmother's beach cottage on Fire Island when they unexpectedly dropped the steak in a pail of blue dye. Screaming disaster, they rushed the steak into the ocean and gave it a good washing. Much to their surprise it was the tastiest steak ever.

◆

George V. Wright, "Cuisine Sauvage," Travelers' Tales Food:
A Taste of the Road

VI

$\mathcal{I}$NTO A $\mathcal{D}$ESERT $\mathcal{P}$LACE

Be prepared.
—*Boy Scout motto*

———

THERE ARE DARK CORNERS IN THE WORLD. Far away from the wines of France, Italy, and California, removed from the hedonistic tables of Thailand and Malaysia, hidden from the culinary lights of China, I've seen the wastelands stretch in their lonely expanse. These desert places are home to people who care little for what they eat, as long as they fill their bellies and make no demands on their senses. You, O Fearless One, surely know of some of these places: Central Africa, Turkmenistan, Detroit. They are not physical deserts, but deserts of gustatory creativity.

We may travel to these barren desert places for many good reasons. Perhaps a great adventure awaits us. Maybe our ancestors came from there, or perhaps we are enamored of its literature. I go to England because of its historical value, and its place as the font of mainstream American culture. But I've never heard anyone utter the words, "Let's go to England for the food!" People go to Russia to see the ballet and Tolstoy's grave, but nobody goes there for black bread and borscht. You could get better in New York anyway. Costa Rica for the rainforest or Tanzania for a photo safari? Sign me up. But for dinner? Not a chance.

Among the most frustrating of the desert places are those that are so close geographically, yet so far culturally, from great gastronomic neighbors. How is it that England

and France lie 21 miles apart, on the same latitude, with the same type of soil and similar climate, and yet...and yet. How often during a year's sojourn in the U.K. did I gaze longingly across the channel and sigh?

More surprising still is India. There in the center of one of the world's great culinary schools, most of the food eaten by most of the people most of the time is bland, bland, bland. And though it is the land of spice, spices are relatively expensive and most of the people are poor. But India I can understand to some degree. It is not a café society. It is a domestic society. Entertaining and gastronomy take place at home. There is no tradition of dining in public. Consequently, there is no substitute for being invited home to dinner.

It can be especially hard in northern India where every restaurant seems to have the same menu. The cuisine is limited by several factors: narrow range of ingredients, and for many people, no meats, cheeses, wines, beer, fish, or vinegar. Even vegetables seem limited to okra, spinach, cauliflower, eggplant, and peas.

I love the bread in Pakistan and northern India where it is cooked in open tandoori ovens. For about one rupee, I can watch the bread vendor throw dough onto the surface of the hearth, the bread bubble and turn brown, and the vendor peel the bread from the stone surface. Within minutes it's ready, hot from the oven, chewy and delicious.

◆

Cailín Boyle, writer, San Francisco, California

And how often have they come to me looking like wilted weeds rather than the greengrocer's pride? The traditional fuel is cow dung, which doesn't burn hot or long, so there is little or no deep frying, baking, searing, or barbecue. And who would want spicy ribs done over a cow flop anyway?

If you're reading this book it's because, like me, you care enough about what you eat to be willing to do something about it. Even in a desert place. Sometimes you can do a lot, sometimes only a little. But do what you can, and you'll reap your reward. As we did in the Golden Triangle, somewhere in Burma, or Thailand, or Laos. It's hard to say exactly where.

We were struggling up some of the steepest hills I have ever climbed. And there were no switch-back trails. It was all just straight up! As I labored behind our guide I could see the huge muscles of his calves that seemed to propel him effortlessly upward. Mine were puny by comparison, and I wondered if they would even get me to wherever he was leading us.

Hill followed ever higher hill as we put the jungle lowland behind and below us. My body ached with the effort, and the sweat poured down my face in cascades. Once I thought I might faint, so I dropped to the ground and guzzled the last of my water. "How much farther?" I gasped to our guide.

"Not far," he said easily. He always said, "not far."

When I thought I could not possibly go any farther, I looked across a grassy field to see a woman in a blue Hmong dress tending the white opium poppies that grew there. "Not far. Not far," our guide called to us. We passed through the field, and by the woman, who stopped her work to smile a greeting, up a final slope, and arrived at a self-contained village of Hmong farmers.

Carnation Milk's the best in the lan'
It comes to you in a li'l red can.
No tits to pull, no hay to pitch
Jes punch a hole in the sonofabitch.

♦

Anonymous

They were surprised, though pleased, to see a trio of *farang* stagger into their midst, and quickly set us down to tea and rice cakes. In this desert place, that's about as elaborate as the Hmong get. We reciprocated with three large bottles of beer we had lugged along. The people were amazed at this. They had heard of beer, but they were so far back of beyond that they had never even seen, let alone tasted, the stuff. We poured it into bowls and they watched it gurgle and foam up to the rims. They passed it among themselves, sipping, sniffing, and exchanging eager remarks. Then, in the *pièce de résistance,* we astonished them even further with our final offering: cheese and tomato sandwiches. After consuming them, they said we were the most welcome guests they had ever had, and that we should come and visit them any time we liked. And they marked the occasion by offering us the pipe, and a bit of the poppy harvest.

TIPS

➤ Carry something good to drink. I carry two half-bottles of California wine. Half-bottles are less likely to break, and I can carry a red and a white. It's not only a godsend in a culinary wasteland, it's a good remedy for homesickness and a

I always stash some of my favorite tea in a pocket of my luggage. A little comfort and familiarity of home for my soul and my stomach. It helps in soothing the mind and body in unfamiliar territory. Chamomile to help me sleep, mint for minor stomach upset, rose hip just because I like it, and green tea, because it's a taste of home and family for me. I grew up in Japan, and it is often the comforts of home and childhood that one seeks when in a strange place.

◆

M. Midori, *professional domina and fetish diva, San Francisco, California* good way to make a new friend by sharing. And stock up on those lovely little liquor packets in East Africa. (See Chapter IX.)

➤ Carry your favorite tea. Even in East Asia you can get some pretty sorry tea. Before there were tea bags, tea was pressed and molded into the shape of small bricks about the size and shape of a deck of cards, for shipment. Today, this is how the finest luxury teas are found, embossed with the producer's seal. Because the brick shape reduces the surface area, little is exposed to air, making it especially suitable for travel and long shelf life. You just break off a tiny piece to make a cup.

➤ A friend of mine, Bob Okumura, carries his own gourmet coffee and a one cup electric coffee maker with all the necessary adapters. It once kept the two of us sane in the coffee desert that is rural Indochina. You can get the coffee in pressed bricks, just like the tea. (See Resources and References chapter.)

➤ I generally don't recommend carrying "survival food" or mountaineering rations. For the most part they are canned food in flexible packages, or

───── ⁂ ─────

Having found ourselves in London one Valentine's Day, we built ourselves a lovers' feast from the selection at Harrod's Food Halls and brought it back to the hotel. We had no problem finding a good wine, two glasses, and a corkscrew as well. Back in the hotel, we got comfy, sipped wine, and ate foie gras, English Stilton, Italian bread, prosciutto, marinated artichokes. And for dessert, petit fours and coffee with sorbet, and...well.... One of my favorite meals ever.

◆

Céline Fleur, engineering documentation specialist, San Francisco, California

dehydrated stuff that tastes like it. Of course, if you are in the middle of nowhere and all that is available is boiling water, it can carry you through to the next way station.

➤ Carry a tin of superior paté, smoked salmon, or potted cheese. Or peanut butter, which keeps well. A little goes a long way with bread or crackers, or even rice.

➤ Be self-reliant. Don't count only on restaurants. Go to the local markets and buy things that you can prepare in your hotel or a picnic area. Carry a cloth or mesh bag with you for the purpose.

➤ Of course you already carry a Swiss army or other multipurpose knife. Throw in a vegetable peeler too.

➤ Carry a Tupperware bowl. When you're dying for salad in a place like India, go to market and buy cucumbers, tomatoes, onions, lemons or limes, salt, and pepper. Then to the Ayurvedic medicine store for olive oil. Peel and slice the veggies, mix all together, and Voila!, a feast of roughage which your body will thank you for.

> *Normally, airline meals are chosen for ease of serving and consuming. But once, I was served a large pork chop, which I ate with a Swiss Army knife and a screwdriver because the plastic cutlery wasn't up to the job. Ever since, I've always traveled with a knife and fork in my flight bag.*
>
> ◆
>
> Keith Kellett, writer,
> Salisbury, England

➤ Some experienced travelers I've met pack a small can of condensed milk. It's useful in rural areas where the coffee has no cream or the porridge comes without milk. Poured

over chopped fresh fruit it makes a nourishing breakfast. I've even seen it used as trade goods, swapped for
a whole fresh pineapple.

➤ Carry your own hot sauce. Even in India. I'm serious!

➤ In a capital city go to the U.S. Embassy and chat up
one of the Marine guards. They are often friendly, or at
least polite, and they know all the best places in town
up to a certain price range. If you're really lucky (and
attractive women tend to be), you just might get invited
to the Marine House. Its "recreation area" will often
have a name like *The Red Dog Saloon*, and in a desert
place it can be the
jumpin'est joint in town.

➤ If you are going on a
trek or safari, make sure
you first get recommen-
dations for the operator,
and let him know you
want to eat well. Some
are quite good at pro-
viding victuals. Others
are more lax.

➤ Prowl the back streets
and follow your nose.
Don't be scared.
Whenever people are
serving food, they're
not trying to hurt you.

➤ Desperate for a real
meal in such dark corners as Khartoum, New Delhi,
Moscow? Most international class hotels offer a lun-

> ——— \\\|// ———
>
> *My husband and I went on a
> camel safari in the Thar Desert
> in Rajusthan, India. Our guide
> cooked for us every night under
> the stars. During the day while
> trekking through villages, he'd
> stop at a local "store" to buy
> ginger and garlic and other
> perishables while the villagers
> gathered around and stared at
> us in amazement. Once or
> twice our guide jumped off the
> camel cart with an empty bottle
> and disappeared into a field to
> milk a passing goat!*
>
> ◆
>
> Jackie Taylor, "Cooks Forum,"
> Compuserve

cheon buffet. They can cost as little as $10 and such a feed can really boost your spirits when they've been laid low by one too many meals of what seem like famine relief rations.

➢ If you're there for a long haul, have something nice shipped from home. Anyone who has been a student abroad, in the military or the Peace Corps, will remember how uplifting a "care package" is.

➢ Plan ahead. Know your terrain. Ask people who have been there, consult the guidebooks, speak to the tourist bureau. There's no substitute for knowing the lay of the gastronomic land, especially when the pickings will be slim.

➢ You can always depend on potatoes wherever you find them.

➢ Wherever you are, don't be shy about asking for something not on the menu. Oftentimes, especially in non-industrial countries, if they don't happen to have it, they'll go get it for you. Or if you bring it to them, they'll cook it for you. On a fishing expedition to

_____ ◟◟◟◟◟ _____

It had been a long day of horseback riding and mule-packing through rugged, but magnificent terrain, on the fourth day of a week-long class called "Survival in the Wilderness with Livestock." I was feeling tired and hungry, too long deprived of creature comforts. Somehow the cook served an impossible feast at the 8,000-foot level of the High Sierras: roast leg of lamb, complete with mint jelly and cheesecake for dessert. With my hunger satisfied, other senses called and what followed was an equally delicious tryst under the stars in the bedroll of Cowboy Fred. The moral? Savor deprivation. It makes the senses sharper and the satisfactions sweeter.

◆

Kat Sunlove, publisher,
Spectator Magazine,
Emeryville, California

Mexico we brought our excess catch to a restaurant and offered them the lot if they would provide a meal at no charge for the six of us. Win-win situation.

➤ Above all, try to concentrate on what's good locally. Remember, you aren't going to Central America to get a great Tempura. Every place has something to offer (with the possible exception of the Central African Republic). England has good beer; Russia good bread and ice cream; the fish on Costa Rica's Caribbean coast is excellent; the Polish do well with duck and the Finns are good with fish. Find the veins of excellence and mine them!

> _____ ␣ \\\\\\// _____
>
> _We were on the Don Jose, Baja Expeditions' 14-passenger vessel on the Sea of Cortez. With my guidebook Spanish I tried to convey my "dietary preferences" to the cook. "Sin carne," I tried. "Sin queso. Sin grasa." He did pretty well. Kept the meat from my sopa and the chicken from my ensalada. Really outdid himself one noon with shredded carrot quesadillas. Strange, but very tasty._
>
> ◆
>
> _Marilyn Pribus, teacher,_
> _Fair Oaks, California_

➤ Throughout the British Isles there are two things on which you can always depend: breakfast and afternoon tea. (Pubs can also be a good source, but it can be hit or miss.) The English, Scots, and Irish like to start the day with a monster feed of porridge, bacon, kippers or kidneys, sausage, eggs any style, toast with excellent butter and jam, smoked salmon, grilled tomatoes, fried potatoes…. Afternoon tea is a proper potful, served with buns, scones, biscuits, marmalade, sometimes smoked or potted meats. Who needs dinner after all that?

➤ Any place in the Chinese or Indian schools of cuisine is a good place to practice vegetarianism. Especially the Indian state of Tamil Nadu.

➤ If you are anywhere near a brewery, winery, or distillery, or a coffee, tea, or spice plantation, it will likely be open to visitors. Go. You are the kind of person such enterprises exist for and the operators will usually be happy to see you. They will also, by virtue of their work, be in a good position to give you advice on where to find the best places to eat, sleep, and visit.

> *Sometimes you just have to accept the inevitable, and suffer. Four friends and I had hired a private railway car in Burma. It had sleeping and lounge quarters, bath, deck, and kitchen with the services of a cook. Or as our travel agent in Rangoon assured us in a fax, the kitchen was complete with "cock service." As it happened, our "cock" did not, generally, prove useful, beyond keeping the beer moderately cold. A lady in our party, frustrated with the "service," proclaimed that "Our cock sucks!"*
>
> ◆
>
> *Bob Okumura, banker, San Francisco, California*

➤ On airplanes, trains, and buses, you are perfectly at liberty to bring your own food. Visit a deli or the local market to supply your sky high picnic or rolling feast. If the market is bare and there is no deli in town, many hotels can easily put together a basket for you.

➤ Most airlines offer alternatives to their normal meals, e.g. kosher, vegetarian. They are usually superior. You need to call at least 24 hours ahead of time to arrange for them.

GUSTATORY GOALS

➤ Do the wild and crazy. When trekking across Tibet, if you go native you'll be living on barley meal and yak butter tea. If you don't go native you'll likely be living on freeze-dried and canned food. Carry the means to produce one superior feast to brighten your darkest culinary hour in your tattered tent on the high plateau. The juxtaposition of a great feast in a gastronomic desert will give you, Fearless Diner, some of the most delicious antithesis you will ever know. You might try a menu of steak with green peppercorn sauce, basmati rice, marinated vegetables, and red wine.

I avoid ethnic restaurants in countries where nobody of that particular ethnicity actually lives. Chinese restaurants in Ireland, for example. Now, I might get lucky, but if I order twice-cooked pork and the waiter asks if I'd like rice or french fries with that, it may be time to make my way politely toward the exit.

◆

*Danny Carnahan, musician,
Berkeley, California*

Carry with you:
    1 small can green peppercorns
    2 ounces brandy
    1 bottle superior red table wine (Zinfandel is good
        with this dish)
    1 package basmati rice
    1 jar marinated green beans, baby eggplants, or
        other vegetable
    1 teaspoon dried tarragon

In Tibet purchase:

Yak steak
Yak butter
Yak cream
1 onion

This plan works just as well in other places, and with any of the three schools.

➤ Make it a point to taste something wholly unfamiliar. And when you do, savor that first moment. It will never come again. Some suggestions.

- an exotic fruit
- camel's milk
- blood sausage
- fried insects
- fermented, pickled, or putrefied (seriously) parts of animals
- heirloom grains or beans
- edible flowers
- rare wines
- an unfamiliar spice

➤ Some of the world's culinary deserts: this list is chosen for its geographical representation; it is far from complete. And no ax was ground in its making. I've left a few blank lines for you to fill in your favorites.

• Arkansas	• Israel	• Turkmenistan
• Balkans	• Mongolia	•
• Borneo	• Peru	•
• Chad	• Russia	•
• Costa Rica	• Slovakia	•
• England	• Sudan	•
• India	• Tanzania	•
• Iran	• Tibet	•

*In Bruge, Belgium I was stopped cold by the sign outside a restaurant:
"Isra-Mex," it announced. "Israeli-Mexican Cuisine." Upon entering, I
smiled gamely at the waitress and asked, "So, your margaritas —are they
kosher?" She shot me back a glance that said, "Yeah, like I haven't heard
that one before." I craved Mexican, but after glancing around the restaurant I had second thoughts. An enchilada at a neighboring table turned out
to be chicken and brie wrapped in pita bread and drowned in what
appeared to be ketchup.*

◆

John Flinn, travel editor, San Francisco Examiner

VII

STRANGE, WONDERFUL, AND TABOO

> All I ask of food is that it doesn't harm me.
> —*Michael Palin*

———

IN PAMPANGA, a small Philippine town, I was traveling to Olongapo City from Manila. I was hungry and had walked into a hole-in-the-wall restaurant, the kind that has a counter for about three and seats for two. The proprietor spoke no English, but I spoke enough Tagalog to say something like, "Give me your best."

He brought me a steaming bowl of something that looked like river bottom mud, the kind that gooshes up between your toes when you walk barefoot in it. Now I had heard that people who live along the Nile and the Amazon sometimes eat the silt from their river bottoms in time of famine. It is said to have a lot of nutrients. I had no problem with that, per se, but I happened to know that the only river for miles around was an open sewer. I asked the man what the dish was, and he said, "*Dinuguan*," but it meant nothing to me. "If it's river silt," I thought, "I hope it's well cooked. Very well cooked."

I took a bite, and even though it had the look and texture of mud, it was delicious. It tasted somewhat like a rich beef stew cooked with a lot of red Bordeaux wine. In the mush, there were also what seemed like little dumplings or big gravy lumps that stuck to the roof of my mouth like peanut butter, but were even more tasty than the surrounding goosh. I had two bowls of it, some rice, and a San Miguel beer, and called that a good meal, whatever it was.

A week later I described the strange, delicious dish to Ricardo Paglinawan, a Filipino friend, and asked him if he knew what it was.

"Oh, sure," he said. "That's blood."

"Blood!?"

"Yeah, blood."

"Blood?"

"Sure. They make it from duck's blood, or pig's blood. It's like a blood soup. So you liked it, eh?"

"Blood? You mean they flavor the soup with blood?"

"No, they just cook some blood. Maybe they put some salt in it, but mainly, it's just blood."

"But...but...what about the little...the little lumps? What were the lumps?"

"Oh, sometimes they cook it too fast and it clots. So you liked it?"

> ───── ⋅⋚⋛⋅ ─────
>
> The Fafaru Effect: "Sometimes it helps to close your eyes," was Kate Browne's anthropological advice to me as we contemplated the concoction of fish fermenting in a gourd of sea water. Indeed, the culinary specialties of remote places, such as this miasmic delicacy of the Austral Islands, often assail rather than seduce the senses. But closing the eyes immediately reduces sensory intake by twenty percent, can be mistaken for ecstasy, and may easily serve as the prelude for a swoon.
>
> ◆
>
> Jane Albritton, editor, Denver, Colorado

Well, yes, I did like it. I will confess I liked it more when I didn't know what it was, but I did like it, and still do, damn it!

No matter what part of the world you come from, if you travel widely, you are going to encounter food that is unusual, strange, maybe even immoral, or just plain weird.

Of course "strange" depends upon your point of view. To the Eskimo (Inuit) a vegetarian diet is strange. He needs his raw meat and blubber. A native of the Himalayas would recoil at the site of lobster or crab. The Chinese turn up their noses at cheese, thinking it barbarous food for barbarous people. The Australians eat *vegemite*, a cultured yeast product that tastes like salted toe jam. Many people around the world find peanut butter disgusting.

Long ago I adopted a rule for strange encounters, and it has become my motto: wherever I go, whatever people I visit, I bow to their kings, respect their gods, and eat their viands no matter what. There is *nothing* I will not eat or drink at least once. And if I don't eat it a second time, it will only be because I don't like the taste; aesthetics be damned. I am a culinary Pagan, and I worship at every altar.

"Real men don't eat quiche," they say. Bah! Real men eat what they damn well please! A food is nutritious and wholesome or it isn't; it's tasty or it isn't; and that's all I worry about. Through taste and smell I partake of Humanity's and Nature's infinite variety. A willing palate and an open mind will open a world of discovery to you. Of course some things will take a bit of getting used to, but the efforts are small and the rewards are great: fun, adventure, good eating, warm memories, and the useful wisdom that there are no gross foods, only gross feeders.

That said, we also do well to be aware of local taboos and religious proscriptions. Even as a friendly gesture, the offer of a pork chop to a Muslim will not score you any points. There are people in the world who will feast on dog meat stew but are revolted by a rare beefsteak. And there are still parts of the world where the dearly departed must not be spoken of in a culinary context. Be wise, be informed, be respectful, and discreet. But above all, be bold!

TIPS

➤ In Thailand deep fried giant locusts are a popular snack. They are high in protein, low in cholesterol, and cheap. And remember, John the Baptist lived on them.

> _____ ⟋⟍⟋⟍ _____
>
> *When sampling crispy Mexican grasshoppers, I choose the smallest size. That way I can focus on how they taste instead of how they look.*
>
> ◆
>
> *Margo True, staff editor,* Gourmet, *New York*

➤ The Chinese believe that shark fin soup is a potent aphrodisiac, and serve it at wedding feasts and to the tired and timid. If you order this in the presence of your Chinese hosts, and remark authoritatively on the soup's special powers, it would be the equivalent of a Chinese peasant capably holding forth on the merits of this year's Beaujolais.

➤ Sam Seh is a Chinese white wine with a whole snake in the bottle, usually a pit viper and highly poisonous in its live state. (Remember the worm in a bottle of Mescal?) Soused, as it is in the bottle, it is rendered benign. Like so many other things the Chinese eat and drink, it is said to revive the lagging libido. Drink a toast with this stuff to establish your bona fides. (And yes, you can eat the worm in the bottle of Mexican Mescal.)

➤ Chinese cooks revere the thousand year egg. A chicken or duck egg is wrapped in lime clay for about eight weeks. The lime leaches through the eggshell and into the white and yolk, turning them blue and green respectively, and hardening them to barely hard boiled. The taste is somewhat fishy with buttery overtones. If you enjoy it, or seem to, your Chinese friends will approve.

➤ Filipinos enjoy a special egg dish called *balut*. A duck egg is allowed to incubate just until the embryo is neither egg nor meat, then is baked in a moist heat. Broken open the perfect *balut* reveals a yolk with numerous blood vessels, and the mere suggestion of bones and feathers which will disintegrate at a touch. It's especially good with a cold San Miguel beer.

➤ In Laos don't pass up the chance to eat fire ant soup. Formic acid coating the bodies of the ants gives the soup a wonderful tangy flavor. Try it at the Sukvemarn restaurant in Vientiane.

_____ ⑊ _____

In Taiwan, when you buy a movie ticket, if you have hunger pangs, you may not want to enter the theater empty handed—the older theaters have no concession stands. But, somewhere near the ticket window there should be a little stand selling the traditional Taiwanese idea of savory movie treats. These will include pickled duck tongues—these are good; small rice cakes made with chicken blood—not a lot of flavor actually; ribbons of seaweed; tofu; and thousand year eggs, pungent opaque greenish-black on the inside— lots of flavor, maybe too much for some. The vendor will also sell canned teas, sodas, and Taiwan Beer—most notable for its incredibly drab can.

◆

Mark Cannon, television writer, Los Angeles, California

➤ Throughout tropical Asia you can find restaurants that cater to tourists whose menus offer "steak." Be advised that unless the "steak's" origin is cited, it's likely to be water buffalo. But it's not all that bad.

➤ Invited home to dinner in Kuwait, if you se
slaughtered sheep carcass hanging at the en[
have been much honored. The beast will be

➤ In Egypt it is very easy and convenient to hire a camel
and go trekking across the desert. It is equally easy to
go to the butcher's and get a few pounds of camel for
dinner. It's highly prized, and justly so.

➤ Sweets in India are shockingly, shudderingly, make-
your-teeth-hurt sweet.

➤ In Latin America, as in Latin Europe, no part of a cow
goes unused. In addition to sweetbreads, organ meats,
and entrails (chitterlings, or chitt'lins), expect to
encounter grilled cow's udder, fried bull's testicles,
sautéed veal brains, stewed spinal cord, and blood
sausage. I've had them
all and they've all been
artfully prepared and
very tasty.

➤ In Poland, as in the
Philippines, people
enjoy a soup made of
duck's or pig's blood. It
contains nearly all the
vitamins, minerals and
other nutrients a person
requires. It's close to a
perfect food. In East
Africa, the lion hunting
Masai tribe live almost exclusively on cow's blood and
milk. Fearless as they are, they don't even cook the

_We finally had the ant eggs at
Cien Años restaurant in
Tijuana, and they were divine.
Came on top of a steak, which
was a waste of good ant eggs, so
we ordered an entire plate and
just stuffed them in our mouths
with our fingers. Like eating
very crunchy garlic air. Yum!_

♦

_Paula McDonald, writer,
San Diego, California_

blood. They either drink it straight, or mix it with milk. If you're ever offered a gourd full of this stuff, you don't have to actually drink it. But you must at least show your appreciation by touching it to your lips. Cheers. (Psst. It really isn't bad.)

➤ If you actually have the opportunity to see sausage being made, don't.

➤ The bold (or crazy) Japanese gourmand really does eat "Fugu," the toxic liver of the puffer fish. Specially trained and government-certified chefs prepare it in such a way that only a trace of the tetradotoxin remains to cause the mouth to tingle and the diner to know the thrill of dancing with Death. But sometimes Death decides to lead. The Japanese press reports about 300 such tangos per year. Cross this one off your dance card.

——— 〰 ———

Haggis, *a sheep's stomach filled with oatmeal, entrails and a splash of whiskey, then steamed or boiled, is Scotland's most traditional dish. Immortalized by the celebrated poet Robert Burns, the haggis was presented, with the accompaniment of a piper, to the head of the household. The recipient would thrust a dirk (traditional Scottish knife) into the haggis and serve it along with neeps (turnips) and tatties (potatoes). I recommend Chivas Brothers The Century of Malts, the very spirit and essence Scotland, as a suitable partner to the enduring haggis. It will make a believer of you.*

♦

Jim Cryle, whiskey lover, Aberdeen, Scotland

➤ If you still think sushi is weird, where in hell have you been?!

➤ The most astonishing tropical fruit anywhere is the durian. A melon-like fruit with a yellow, pudding-textured flesh, its odor is best described as pig shit, turpentine, and onions garnished with a dirty gym sock. It can be smelled from yards away. Despite its great local popularity, it is forbidden to eat durian on the subway in Singapore.

➤ Anywhere in the South Pacific, refrain from talking of cannibalism. The popular term for human flesh is *long pig*, for its taste being similar to pork. If anyone should ever call you a *long pig*, get the hell outta Dodge.

I've always eaten avocados as guacamole, or in a salad with salt and pepper, the usual seasoning. I thought that was the only way. Imagine my surprise in Brazil when I saw people enjoying them as a shake with milk and sugar!

◆

Rosa Carmelita, engineer, San Francisco, California

➤ The Muslim dietary code is fairly simple. Pork is strictly forbidden, as is animal blood. Alcohol is only advised against, and most Muslim countries do not outlaw it. Food conforming to Muslim law is called Khalal. In countries with large Muslim populations food stalls often use two colors of plates: green for serving Khalal; orange for all else.

➤ The Jewish dietary code is elaborate. Its chief features are: proscription against pork, blood, invertebrates, scavengers, and carnivores; meat and dairy cannot be present on the same plate.

➤ The word *kosher* means "fit." If something is called *kosher*, it fits in with the law of *Kashrut*, which governs numerous aspects of Jewish life, including what is fit to eat.

➤ Hindus are not strictly prohibited from eating beef,

but the vast majority elect not to as cow worship is central to their religion and killing a cow is an offense in much of India.

➤ In India, don't go into a Jain temple if you have just eaten garlic, onion, potato, or any other thing that grows underground. These things, along with all animal products, are forbidden to the Jains.

GUSTATORY GOALS

➤ In England you won't find much in the way of strange fare. But you will find strange names for their favorite dishes. Spotted Dick, Toad in the Hole, Bubble and Squeek, Starry Gazy Pie, to name a few. See what else you can find. And do they look and taste like their names?

➤ In West Africa, monkey is highly regarded and

Certain members of the Agudat Yisrael party in the Israeli parliament tried to ram a law down the throats of Israelis that would forbid the sale of pork to anyone but Christians. Some more secular Jews countered with a gastronomic demonstration: a free lunch of ham sandwiches. As one supporter at the unkosher repast said, "I've never touched pork, but once you let these Agudat characters into your sandwiches, they'll want to climb into bed with your wife as well."

◆

Sam Bagdikian, restaurateur,
New York

My vote for the Australian "national dish" goes to the Pie Floater. This is a heated meat pie, served in a bowl of pea soup. A pie-cart operator told me that his pie floaters were the cheapest dinner anywhere in town. This was probably just as well for his "pitch" was right outside the Adelaide Casino.

◆

Keith Kellett, writer,
Salisbury, England

available in many restaurants. But you generally have to order it special. It tastes a lot like pork. Order it barbequed on a stick. That way you won't have to look him in the face.

➤ In the Philippines there are restaurants that specialize in dog flesh. You won't see them advertised as such, and you'll have to coax your Filipino friends into taking you to one since they know that we don't eat the canine here in the West. But go ahead and break the taboo over there. The Filipinos claim that it prevents tuberculosis. And I confess I've never seen a Philippine dog with TB.

So far in West Africa I'd eaten bush rat, dik dik, monkey, and goat, but I couldn't figure out the animal that was in this stew. It was thick-skinned, and the woman who dished it out watched as I chewed, and chewed, and chewed, and laughed when I finally spit it out. "What is it?" I mimed, because she spoke only Woloof. It really was delicious, but there were these hunks of skin, really, an inch thick and like tire rubber. "What is it?" I asked the woman again. She brightened, and mimed pin pricks poking her arm. Great. Now I can add porcupine to my litany of exotic dishes in Africa.

◆

Carla King, writer, San Francisco, California

If you're prone to nausea when swallowing slimy slugs or crunching beetles, pack your own plastic bag. If your host looks aghast, explain that it was so good you're taking some home in a doggie bag for later, it's an old American custom.

◆

Brenda Love, writer, Hillsborough, California

VIII

$\mathscr{S}$TAYING $\mathscr{H}$EALTHY
AND $\mathscr{F}$IT

Keep a tight asshole.
—*Norman Mailer,* The Naked and the Dead

———

A PRINCIPAL OBJECT IN TRAVEL is to broaden the mind without loosening the bowels. I am aware of the dangers wherever I go and take necessary precautions. But by simply going on the journey I also take necessary risks. I'm no doctor, so I can't give you any professional medical advice. However, I can tell you of my own experience, and let you be the judge.

I've been traveling the wide world since 1971 and I have been laid low a time or two by gastroenteritis, the catch-all term for Traveler's Bellyache, Montezuma's Revenge, or The Green Apple Quickstep. I've also suffered from jungle rot, scabies, crabs, and...uh...other maladies. If you travel, you may get sick a little. Even going from one clean, modern, industrial democracy to another, the mere change in the mineral balance of the water, combined with jet lag can bring on the bellyache. And I remember the time I spent a month in Mexico with no problem, but coming home I stopped in Los Angeles for two days and fell violently ill! The combined effects of bad air, heavy traffic, and fast food. Well, that's my theory.

One stratagem I use to avoid getting sick (and I reiterate that this is not professional medical advice, just my own experience) is to carry a broad spectrum antibiotic, usually tetracycline, which is available over the counter in many countries. If I think I'm in danger, I take 500 milligrams in the morning, and 500 milligrams at night. I haven't been sick in years. Except for Los Angeles.

Many doctors would advise you not to use such a drug prophylactically. In certain individuals unpleasant side effects can occur, such as indigestion, yeast infection, sun sensitivity, and even caffeine nerves. In extreme cases they can cause tendon damage, and can interact dangerously with other drugs. I know from experience and medical feedback what I can take and what I can't.

I have suffered one nasty side effect from this stratagem: I am likely to be the only man in the history of tourism to have traveled the length and breadth of India and suffered not diarrhea, but constipation! Four days of feasting and I had nothing to show for it. And all the while my two traveling companions were suffering from the more usual ailment. I made mighty efforts, and many prayers to John, but they availed me nothing. My lips began to turn blue. India is no place to find laxatives. I was on the verge of sucking pond water, anything to get some action going. In desperation I went to

———— \\\\\\// ————

A must in my medicine kit is a box of Chinese herbal medicine called the curing pill. My acupuncturist/herbalist turned me on to them. You take this small vial filled with brown pills the size of lead shot. They taste like dirt. But I find that for me it's the best medicine for most gastrointestinal unpleasantries. The info from one of the boxes: CURIN WAN natural herb food supplement. Ingredients: Wheat flour, pollen, tangerine, coix barley, arrowroot, beefsteak leaf, angelica seed, magnolia bark, rice plant leaf, chrysanthemum, hoelen mushroom and peppermint with natural flavorings. It comes 10 vials per box.

♦

M. Midori, professional domina and fetish diva, San Francisco, California

the food stalls of the nearby village and began to eat *dahl,* spinach, potatoes, fruit, whole wheat bread, any and all forms of dietary fiber I could find. I waited until the next day and downed a half-gallon of strong coffee and took a brisk walk. The results were said to have been recorded by an Indian Geological Survey seismic research station. If you follow my example of using antibiotics, be warned. And be aware that there is a variety of opinion among physicians on the wisdom of using antibiotics prophylactically, and that I don't rely on it exclusively; I still take the standard precautions as well.

Your guidebook to your destination should have all the specifics about the local diseases and how to avoid them, and what vaccinations are required. It should also give you the standard spiel about peeling your fruits and vegetables, making sure your cooked foods are hot off the stove, and avoiding salads and ice cream where appropriate. Read it. And read it again. Then don't despair. Most traveler's ailments are short-lived and more inconvenient than severe. However some, such as giardia, can be life threatening. But so can driving the freeway at home. So go. Have a good time. Eat, drink, be fearless. Just don't be foolish.

While traveling the world, exercise is important. One of the best ways I've found to exercise, eat, drink, and meet new people all at the same time is to hook up with the Hash House Harriers. Begun in 1938 at the Selangor Club of Kuala Lumpur in what was then British Imperial Malaya, this is arguably the oldest, and certainly the largest, international running club in the world. "The Hash" has 1100 chapters worldwide in nearly every capital city and in such far-flung places as San Francisco, Turkmenistan, and the South Pole. And it all began as an excuse to work up a thirst for beer and a hunger for the local food.

They meet once a week, customarily at 5:00 p.m. or 6:00 p.m. on Mondays (it varies here and there), to run a "paper chase." One member is the "hare" who runs ahead leaving a trail of paper bits or chalk marks to show the route, but deviously interwoven with many false trails that can take the pursuers, the "harriers," through muddy ditches, cow pastures, or city streets. It's noncompetitive, recreational,

> _____ ʻ\||/ʻ _____
>
> *Richard Sterling took me to my first Hash in Vientiane, Laos. I can report that even the beer drinking was good exercise, of its kind.*
>
> ♦
>
> *Joe Cummings, guidebook author, Todos Santos, Mexico*

and wholly irreverent. The run is followed by wacky ceremonies, beer, food, and revelry. The Hashers like to call themselves "drinkers with a running problem." As they say, "If you have half a mind to try hashing, that's all you need." Visitors and new members are always welcome.

International hash directories can be had by contacting an Australian embassy or one of the following:

Harrier International Magazine
G.P.O. Box 1670
Bangkok, 10501
Thailand

Interhashional News
10871 Charbono Point
San Diego, CA 92131-1505

TIPS

➤ You might minimize your foolishness and maximize your fearlessness by carrying some traveler's insurance. Knowing that if you need a little medical help to get you through the day and that you can get it easily, can take a lot off your mind. Find yourself a policy that includes helicopter and jet evacuation if you are traveling to a remote or otherwise difficult place.

➤ Don't let yourself get run down. Your immune system may be weakened when you're tired, so pace yourself and get sufficient rest. Practice the art of doing nothing on a regular basis. It's not just good for your body, but can do wonders for your spirit.

➤ In hot climates, don't let yourself get dehydrated. Carry water with you all the time. And don't wait for the sensation of thirst to tell you it's time for a drink. That sensation is very often much delayed.

➤ Beer and soft drinks are generally safe to drink, even in the dirtiest environments. But don't rely on beer (sigh) to keep you hydrated. Alcohol is a diuretic and you'll just piss away the benefits. The sweet drinks can also be deceiving. You'll gulp down a bottle of soda pop in a faraway place and will end up being thirstier than ever.

➤ Carry some iodine tablets to purify water. Then you and your companions can have fun contests to see who produces the most colorful urine.

➤ If iodine is not your cup of tea, invest in a hand-held water filter pump. They are no larger than a shaving kit, they can be had for about $25, and their filters are so fine that some of them can take the color out of coffee. The one thing they can't do is take the odor out of Saigon tap water. Phew!

➤ Carry some fizzies or some powdered drink or vitamin mix to make that stinky water palatable.

➤ Know thy teeth. Get them checked before a long trip.

➤ Where the water is suspect, don't even brush your teeth with it. Use bottled water, even beer if you have to.

➤ Even if the water and the food are pure, that kitchen thrall picking his nose and scratching his privates can infect it. And that can happen just as easily at home. If the staff look dirty, take your business elsewhere.

> *I once brushed my teeth with vodka. I was hung over and it almost made me gag. But I felt it was better to gag on vodka than to let the Siberian water into my mouth.*
>
> ◆
>
> *Stella Upsilon Pike, investment counselor, New York*

➤ Never eat anywhere that employs a thin cook! While this is not, of course, a universal truth, it is a reminder to be observant, to be careful not only about *what* you eat, but who prepares it.

> *In Damascus, avoid eating in outdoor cafes around 8 p.m. That's when the street sweepers make their rounds spraying pesticide.*
>
> ◆
>
> *Cailín Boyle, writer, San Francisco, California*

➤ Tainted meat and dairy are among the most common conveyances of filth-to-mouth diseases. You can significantly reduce your chances of getting sick simply by avoiding animal foods. That's a tough choice for a dedicated omnivore, but if you see billows of flies around the local butcher's or fishmonger's, and milk sitting in a hot sun, well, you be the judge.

➤ Papaya enzyme tablets work well for heartburn induced by strange foods. They can be more effective than brand name products such as Tums or Rolaids and are available in health food stores and many of the larger grocery stores.

➤ Pack your own toilet paper or tissues if you are fastidious about what you wipe with. Bring aloe vera to apply to a sore bum should you get the trots.

➤ All the standard precautions notwithstanding, eat and drink as the local people do in those areas where the cuisine is highly developed; but take your own counsel elsewhere. In China people don't eat raw vegetables or salads; they do eat food cut into small pieces and cooked over high heat, and they drink hot water. If I do the same, I likely won't get sick. However, if I were trekking across rural southern Congo I would go on the assumption that the locals are immune to everything and that if I eat like them I'll die.

------ ☀ ------

So the worst has happened. Something you ate has turned on you. Once you reach the bathroom you don't know which end needs attention first. Give your body a chance to get rid of the problem. To help the process along and avoid dehydration, immediately begin drinking water that you know is safe, or a sports drink such as Gatorade. If there's no improvement after 24 hours, take Imodium or other anti-diarrheal. You need medical help as soon as possible if you become lightheaded, weak, dizzy, or your skin stays tented when pinched rather than flattening back to its original surface.

♦

*Bill Baker, R.N.,
Phoenix, Arizona*

------ ☀ ------

In the Cafe of Doubtful Cleanliness, I order hot tea, a hard-boiled egg, a coconut, and an unpeeled banana.

♦

*Kit Snedaker, editor,
Santa Monica, California*

➤ Although my experience of constipation in India is unusual for India, it is not so unusual for travelers generally. It can often be difficult to maintain proper amounts of fiber in the diet when on the road, especially in countries where people eat a lot of fats, meats, or dairy. Nowadays I carry a fiber supplement. I recommend one that comes in tablet form or in individual packets.

> _I've often wondered why more people don't go on exotic trips instead of to outrageously expensive domestic fat farms. I've lost more weight, effortlessly, and learned a lot to boot, in places like Borneo, Togo, and Tibet, than I have staggering around the track back home._
>
> ◆
>
> James O'Reilly, editor and writer, Palo Alto, California

➤ In tropical Asia and Africa, don't assume that because it's sold in a bottle the water is safe to drink. Check to make sure the bottle's seal is intact. I and other travelers have observed water sellers filling Evian bottles from a nearby tap and then selling it as the genuine article.

➤ Vary your gastronomic experience with experience of the local ascetic traditions, such as you would find in a monastery or ashram. Be a diner, and a fearless one, but not an eating machine.

➤ Drink large quantities of water whenever and wherever you can trust it. Tea also works well.

➤ Avail yourself of local fresh fruit. It can be among the best things a place has to offer, and will help to keep you fit, balanced, and regular. Of course, observe all the rules of peeling your fruit.

➤ Some people will think I'm going too far to recommend fasting to food enthusiasts. But the Fearless Diner seeks antithesis. Fasting is especially useful where the food is suspect. It won't hurt you to go hungry for a day, or two, or even three. Just remember to stay hydrated and take your vitamins.

➤ Carry a calorie counter, if you are the sort of person this works for, and use it. Balance your intake with your activity.

➤ Maintain a well-balanced diet according to the food pyramid. Sometimes that's hard to do when on the road, so pay special attention and use vitamin supplements if needed.

➤ Make every meal count as something special. Unless it's a long flight, don't eat on the plane. Don't graze between meals, unless of course it's something like street food in Bangkok. If you've acquired the menu of the evening's restaurant ahead of time, use it to plan your dinner, and delight in the sheer anticipation; it can be almost as tasty as dinner itself, and so low in calories.

➤ Walk. Walk everywhere you can, as often as you can. Get out of the car and walk! It's the most convenient and cheapest way to exercise anywhere. Walk!

➤ If it's too far to walk, rent a bicycle.

➤ Go swimming, in the hotel pool, in the nearby river if it's clean, in the ocean, at the ol' swimmin' hole.

➤ Go dancing. If modern dance or shaking your booty in a disco is not your cup of tea, many ballrooms offer free or inexpensive lessons early in the evening. Shake a leg.

➤ Wherever there are horses, rent one and go riding. It's good exercise, and a fine way to meet folks.

➤ Take along your running shoes and use them. Ask the hotel desk for a good route.

➤ Skip the elevator and take the stairs.

➤ Carry your skipping rope, flexgrips, or other portable exercise equipment.

➤ Basic Hatha yoga postures and breathing exercises, or *t'ai chi* routines, will go a long way towards keeping you calm and flexible on the road. Learn some if you are not already familiar with the basics.

➤ Make time for some kind of *regular exercise*, even if it's only twenty minutes in the morning before sallying forth to feast. You have 24 hours in the day. Your body merits at least 1/3 of 1/24 of that time. Yes, I *know* you're busy, that's why I say *make* time.

➤ Pack a Frisbee. It's good exercise and a good way to meet people in the park.

➤ If you belong to any kind of athletic club or social/business club with athletic facilities, find out if clubs along your route have reciprocal privileges.

➤ When in Calcutta, volunteer for a day or two at Mother Teresa's. It will dull your appetite while you're there. And when you feast again it will be with a sense of reverence for the food and where it came from, and with a sense of gratitude which no spice, no service, no superstar chef could ever give you. You can find Mother Teresa's Missionaries of Charity Mother House at 54A Lower Circular Road, Calcutta.

➤ Many monasteries, temples, and convents of all the world's religions accept visitors and pilgrims. They offer a night's lodging and humble fare for little or nothing. Balance, contrast, variety. I recommend it.

GUSTATORY GOALS

➤ Get enough exercise to stay ravenous.

➤ Get enough sex to stay ravenous.

➤ Take good care of yourself. You're the only one of you we've got.

There is no sauce like a good appetite. And the two best ways I know to work up an appetite are making love and vigorous exercise. The advantages of exercise are that I can do it myself, I don't really have to be in the mood, and if I have a headache, it's afterward, not before. But I'm still hungry. And if you don't know the advantages of making love, well, just keep exercising.

◆

Ilsa Blanston, sculptor, Helena, Montana

IX

DRINK AND BE MERRY

Fill up the bowl then, fill it high,
Fill all the glasses there, for why
Should every creature drink but I,
Why, man of morals, tell me why?
—*Abraham Cowley*, Drinking (1668)

————

SOMEWHERE IN THE HEART OF BORNEO, my buddy
Mack and I found ourselves in the Iban tribal village of
Chief Entili. Our arrival was a sensational event. Only a few
of the people had ever seen a Paleface, and the sudden
appearance of two of them was cause for feasting and
drinking. Accepting the gifts of t-shirts and food we had
brought along, Entili announced that the party should
begin, that liquor should flow, that drummers drum, and
the people dance and sing as much as they desired. We ate
mounds of rice and fried insects. We drank home brew,
men, women, and children alike. In the Iban custom, it is
impolite for a host to allow a guest's cup to empty, and for
the guest to let his cup remain full.

We all got stinking drunk, according to custom, and I
decided to show Chief Entili some feats of acrobatic skill.
I was doing a pretty good, though wobbly, backward som-
ersault when I reached the position where you're standing
on your hands, ready to curl up for another roll back. I was
right near the chief, fairly vertical and head down when I
sort of tipped over sideways and twisted forward and fell
on my face and belly in an attitude of genuflection or kow
tow in front of Entili. It must have looked pretty good, like

I'd done it on purpose. And I'm sure the chief thought the Paleface was putting on a good show. But when I didn't move afterward it was pretty obvious that the booze had got me.

My pal Mack says that's when I began to vomit. He says that I began to push up a mole hill of undigested rice and other goodies right there in front of Entili. Worse, I was doing it on some intricately woven ceremonial mat.

Mack will tell you himself that he was pretty scared, thinking we might lose our heads. He started scooping up my vomit in his hands and running to the windows to throw it out. He kept saying, "I'm sorry! I'm sorry, Chief! I'll clean it up!" Then he'd run back for more, all the while saying, "I'm sorry, please don't be sore." But all the chief did was laugh.

Next morning I sat in a daze in some corner until one of the village women came and found me. She said, "Oh, tsk tsk tsk," and patted me on the shoulder. It's curious how "Oh, tsk tsk tsk" sounds the same in almost any language. She ran and got me some water to drink and a pile of betel nut. She wrapped up several chews for me, then she straightened my hair and wiped my sleep-sodden eyes out with her bare fingers. I couldn't hold back a belch and it became obvious to her that I had a bellyache, lots of gas, and heartburn. She went and got two dried peppercorns, which the people gather in the wild, and crushed them between two small stones then wrapped them in a betel leaf to make a fat pill. The effect was salutary. And I dubbed the woman Doctor Pepper.

So I received a lesson in moderation, and in the fact that customs of the table extend to customs of the bar. A culture reveals itself through drink as well as through food. Traditional toasts often recall moments of historical import ("Next year in Jerusalem"), national longing ("Peace"), occupational solidarity ("To those still at sea"). The imbibing of the national drink is to imbibe one's national identity. And to spend a few hours in the cups with local people is better than any guided tour I can imagine. Many a morning I've woken with a cotton mouth, a throbbing head, and a clutch of new friends. Drinking together

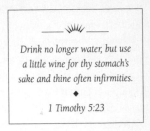

Drink no longer water, but use a little wine for thy stomach's sake and thine often infirmities.

♦

1 Timothy 5:23

can often be a fast track to personal connections and cross-cultural exchange. (I don't want to get any huff-n-puff letters telling me that drinking to excess or driving under the influence are Bad Things. If you've read this far, I assume that you are fearless, not foolish!)

And there is much more to the world of drink than we may be aware. When we think of France or California we usually think of wine; thoughts of Germany bring thoughts of beer; and Scotland conjures up whiskey. But there's no end there. Almost all countries of the world have wineries, breweries, or distilleries. They can be an excellent lens through which to see a region, and provide an entrée to the place not known to the average tourist.

Wherever you go, I recommend a visit to whatever maker of the spirit of Dionysus may be at hand. You will always find there a unique experience of the land you are visiting, one that you cannot duplicate in another country. No two vineyards can produce quite the same wine; no two wells the same beer; no two distilleries the same spirit. When you come away from the Singha brewery in Thailand, the Mondavi winery in California, or the Glenlivet distillery in Scotland you can take away taste and smell memories that bespeak the land with an authority unmatched by any gew-gaws or knick-knacks purchased in a gift shop. And best of all, most tasting rooms charge nothing.

Even most of the predominately Muslim countries have their national drink or favorite import. (Mohammed advises against strong drink, but he does not forbid it.) Egypt produces excellent beer and decent wine; Syria has its licorice-flavored liquor, "Arak"; Indonesian beer is modeled on a good Dutch brew, and many a good Spanish wine is to be had in Morocco.

Guidebooks to many of the drink producers of the world are listed in the Resources and References chapter of this book. And for the world's most extensive drinking and athletic club, read about the "Hash House Harriers" in Chapter VIII. Cheers!

TIPS

➤ In East Africa you can buy shots of liquor in little plastic envelopes that look like packets of ketchup. They fit handily in your pocket or purse, won't easily break, and cost little. They are, in my humble opinion, among the best things ever to come out of Africa. And I find it a source of embarrassment that the land of Yankee ingenuity doesn't have any of them.

The night I arrived in New Delhi, India, I couldn't find a bottle of beer in this Hindu and Muslim town to save my Christian soul. I knew the sons of the Prophet looked down on suds, but I didn't know the followers of Krishna were teetotalers. I came to learn that the Hindus regard alcohol, narcotics, tobacco, and a host of more innocuous things as pollution of the body. Spiritual advancement requires them to keep pure. They can breathe the dirty Delhi air, drink water that would fell a moose, eat fly-bespecked sugar candy by the pound, and walk blithely through acres of excrement, but the brewer's art is pollution. Harumph!

◆

RS

➤ In Anglophone Africa, beer—after the English fashion—is often served at room temperature, and gin and tonic without ice. Even on the equator. Be warned. In a hotel or bar you come to frequent, you can ask ahead of time to have something chilled for you.

➤ You have to be 25 to buy alcohol in India. It's sold in special nondescript stores called "Wine & Beer Shops," though I've never seen wine for sale in them, and beer seems to move slowly. The chief article of commerce here is "Indian-Made Foreign Liquor." Faux Scotch, fake gin, and wannabe brandy are sold by surly, middle-aged louts who slam the bottle on the counter, take your money, and wave you off like a pesky fly. The miscreants don't even give you a bag.

➤ There are "dry states" in India, just as there are "dry counties" in the USA. And there are "dry days" all over the Indian calendar. They usually fall on the hottest and thirstiest days of the year. Be warned.

> *I found that Texas has liquor laws that make drinking there a bit like roving through India. There are "wet" counties, "dry" counties, and some with both wet and dry areas. I had no need for a map of wet vs. dry Texas, though. The dry-wet options tend to fall neatly on either side of an East-West line dividing the pulpit pounders from the bar flies. I just drew a line extending from El Paso in the West to Orange in the East. It was honky-tonk territory below the line and churches above.*
>
> ◆
>
> *Joe Cummings, guidebook author, Todos Santos, Mexico*

➤ In Britain a "Martini" is a glass of vermouth; whiskey is Scotch unless otherwise specified; ordering "on the rocks" gets you a single lump of ice, so ask for more if you want it.

➤ In Poland, if someone looks at you and flicks his finger against his neck, he is inviting you to join him for a drink.

➤ In Russia, vodka bottles are generally not restoppable. If one is opened, it is likely meant to be emptied.

➤ The pouring of wine in Bolivia and Argentina is fraught with ritual and taboo. Let your host or a waiter do it.

➤ Never try to drink more beer than an Australian. And remember that everyone in a drinking group is expected to "shout for a round," i.e. pay in their turn. In traditional pubs you may notice that the bar has no brass rail to put your foot on, but rather a porcelain tile trough with a drain in the middle. In days gone by when the pub closed at 6:00 p.m., it was there for the purpose of

While on a research trek in the Amazon basin I drank what I call "spit in your mouth beer." Women chew grains or roots till they become mushy and saturated with saliva. They spit it into pots, bury them, and let the enzymes in the saliva turn the starches into sugar. Naturally occurring yeast then ferments it. I guess it wasn't too bad. But I wish they could have chilled it.

◆

Rod Johnson, biologist, Peterville, Ohio

"grim, rapid drinking" without losing your place at the bar. Don't pee in it.

➤ The Finns can put it away like nobody's business, so pace yourself. And don't drive afterward. The laws in Finland are strict.

➤ So, the Fearless Diner has fallen into his/her cups and stayed there a bit too long? Well, I'm sorry to say there really isn't any "cure" for a hangover. Some people say you can prevent it by taking lots of vitamins before going to sleep. My advice is, don't go to sleep drunk and you won't wake up with a hangover. But if you do, only time—about twelve hours—will restore you. You can mitigate the effects by rehydrating yourself, eating a little something, taking aspirin, and forcing fluids to flush out your system. Taking "hair of the dog" gives temporary relief, but in the end is counter-productive. So buck up. Take your medicine, suffer your aches, and chalk it up to the price of what I hope will have been one very good time.

➤ If you drink hard liquor before a meal in France, your hosts will shake their heads with that special bemused disdain that they reserve for foreigners.

> ___ ⑊⑊⑊ ___
>
> *We were tasting white burgundies, Montrachet, I think. I was seated next to a young Napa winemaker in rough working clothes. I turned to him and said, "This wine smells like wet sweaters and vomit and wet dog hair." Without missing a beat, he said, "Yeah, it's the bulic acid that gives it that smell." While maintaining a calm exterior, my energy was bubbling up in happiness—for this shared perception of smell had been transmitted with the snap and ease of two pro baseball players warming up; I felt that I had found a soul brother.*
>
> ◆
>
> *George V. Wright, writer and gardener, Bayside, New York*

➤ Germany. Beer. What else can I say? A great deal! Some of the world's greatest wines come from the Mosel and Rhine River valleys.

➢ Local wines, such as Bull's Blood and Tokay, are excellent topics of conversation in Hungary. But don't get into it with the French when in France. Even the most wine ignorant Frenchman thinks he knows more than you and may consider it his civic duty to tutor you. It is safe to suspend this rule when visiting wineries.

➢ Wine is not a drink in Italy; it's a liquid food. Overindulgence is offensive.

➢ Toasts in Sweden are long and formal. Wait until your host has said "Skoal" before taking a drink.

➢ If you want a refill in Japan, hold your glass forth with both hands. And don't refill it yourself. That is done by one's tablemate. The Japanese toast, "*Kampai*," literally means, "Drink it all." Be careful.

➢ Koreans are enthusiastic imbibers and regard drinking together as a good way of establishing friendly relations. But anything you say or promise while you've had a snootful will be taken seriously. There's no taking the Fifth.

> —— ⚝ ——
>
> *In India, if you stick your head into a restaurant and ask if they have beer, they more often than not say, "No." We found a way around this: Walk in and discreetly ask the manager, "If we have a meal here, can you get us a couple of beers?" Nobody ever turned us down. They would sit us in a corner and bring the beers wrapped in paper bags and hide them at our feet under the table, so no one would see our sin.*
>
> ◆
>
> *Paul Harmon, championship dancer, San Jose, California*

➢ Saudi Arabia. Forget it.

➢ If you don't know anything about wine, you will find these books quite helpful: *Wine for Dummies*, by Ed

McCarthy and Mary Ewing-Mulligan and *Adventures on the Wine Route* by Kermit Lynch.

➤ The sommelier (sum-el-yay) is there to advise you. You can rely upon his or her expertise—he knows the restaurant's wine cellar as well as the best choices of wine for the foods you've ordered. Let the wine steward do his job for you.

➤ The Toast originated during the Middle Ages, when people put a piece of scorched bread into a cup of beer or wine for reasons we are no longer sure of. The guest of honor was given the toast when the vessel was emptied. The toast is no longer in the cup, but in the spirit.

➤ Toasts from around the world:

French	*Santé*
Spanish	*Salud*
Italian	*Salute*
German	*Prosit*
Irish	*Slainte*
Russian	*Nazdrovia*
Swedish	*Skoal*
Finnish	*Kippas*
Filipino	*Mabuhay*
Hebrew	*Lachaim*
Japanese	*Kampai*
Chinese	*Gambei*
Dutch	*Prost*
Serbo-Croatian	*Jivili*

GUSTATORY GOALS

➤ Go camping in a remote or wilderness area, and hold a wine tasting. A serious one.

- ➤ Reserve a large table in a fine restaurant and hold a beer tasting. A serious one.

- ➤ Travel through the wine-growing regions of California, France, Italy, or Australia, taste-testing and building up your wine cellar along the way.

- ➤ Select the most romantic, or most beautiful, or most contemplative place you can think of. Go there, and sip your favorite cocktail.

Halfway through the journey on the Orient Express, Gina and I were lounging on the last car of the train, the rear half of which is an open, covered deck. The lush, warm tropical air flowed through the open space and we watched Malaysia recede behind us as we approached Thailand. As I stood sipping a gin & tonic, the sky began to billow with fat monsoon clouds. In moments, sheets of rain were falling, beating a soft tattoo upon the roof. Lightning flashed many times and the thunder roared magnificently. I held my half-finished drink out in the downpour, and within the space of two thunderclaps the glass ran over. I toasted the storm, quaffed the drink, and dubbed it the Monsoon Cocktail.

RS

Here's to you, Fearless One, and a lifetime of
Adventure Eating!

✖
ℛESOURCES AND
ℛEFERENCES

BOOKS FOR FURTHER READING

The Art of Eating by M.F.K. Fisher
New York: Collier Books, 1990

Celebrating Italy by Carol Field
New York: Morrow, 1990
Food customs and festivals of Italy.

Consuming Passions: The Anthropology of Eating
Peter Farb and George Armelagos
New York: Houghton Mifflin, 1980
Why we eat what we eat and how.

Grass Soup by Zhang Xianliang
Lincoln, Mass.: David R. Godine Publisher, Inc., 1995
Dealing with hunger in a Chinese prison camp.

How the Other Half Dies by Susan George
New Jersey: Allenheld, Osmun & Co., 1977
A treatise on starvation.

A Kipper with My Tea by Alan Davidson
San Francisco: North Point Press, 1990
A gastronome's memoirs in the Far East.

Much Depends on Dinner by Margaret Visser
New York: Collier Books, 1988
A history of culinary customs.

A Natural History of the Senses by Diane Ackerman
New York: Vintage, 1990
A lushly written must-read for any person of the senses.

Paris Dreambook by Lawrence Osborne
New York: Vintage Departures, 1990
The darkest guts of Paris.

A Pike in the Basement: Tales of a Hungry Traveler by Simon
Loftus
San Francisco: North Point Press, 1987
A wandering gastronome's recollections.

A Season in Spain by Ann and Larry Walker
New York: Simon & Schuster, 1992
Eating and drinking the Iberian peninsula.

Travels with Lizbeth by Lars Eighner
New York: St. Martin's Press, 1993
Traveling the homeless road and eating from dumpsters.

The Tea Ceremony by Seno Tanaka
New York: Harmony Books, 1977
Comprehensive guidebook to the intricate Japanese ritual.

Won Ton Lust by John Krich
New York: Kodansha, 1997
A search for the best Chinese restaurant in the world.

A Year in Provence by Peter Mayle
New York: Vintage, 1990
Humorous account of a gastronomic year in France.

RESOURCES

The Book of Coffee & Tea by Joel, David, and Karl Schapira
New York: St. Martin's Press, 1975
Everything you ever wanted to know about coffee and tea.

Bugs, Bites & Bowels by Dr. Jane Howarth
London: Cadogan Guides, 1995
Highly readable book on how to stay healthy on the road.

CDC—Centers for Disease Control
Atlanta, Georgia
(404) 639-2572 Travelers' Hotline
(404) 332-4559
(404) 332-4565 (phone line to request written information to be sent via fax)
Up-to-date info on recommended and required inoculations, diseases, symptoms, and their prevention throughout the world.

Dining Customs Around the World by Alice Mothershead
Garrett Park, Maryland: Garrett Park Press, 1982

Encyclopedia of Wine by Frank Schoonmaker
New York: Morrow, 1988
Valuable reference for traveling the wine trail.

Entertainment Discount Guides
(800) 926-0565
For selected cities around the world, a book of discounts ranging from 25% to 50% on hotels, restaurants, dry cleaners, language schools, movies, arts, and entertainment.

Food Festivals: Eating Your Way from Coast to Coast by Barbara Carlson
Detroit: Visible Ink, 1996
Locations, dates, and descriptions of food festivals across the USA.

Goat Gap Gazette
5110 Bayard Ln. #2, Houston TX 77006-6512
(713) 667-4652 days
The "clarion of the chile world," with news for chile-heads about cookoffs, recipes, anecdotes, more.

The Guide to Cooking Schools
Shaw Associates, 1997
625 Biltmore way, Suite 1406, Coral Gables, Florida 33134

(800) 247-6553.
Guide to cooking schools and sponsors of travel programs, plus index of culinary tour & travel programs and
inns, hotels & resorts offering cooking vacations.

Homeopathic Educational Services
Mail order house with catalog of homeopathic books,
remedies, travel and home kits
2124 Kittredge St., Berkeley, CA 94704
(800) 835-9051

*International Brewers' Directory, with Distillers and Soft
Drinks Guide*
Verlag fur Internationale Wirtschaftsliteratur
Bockhornstrasse 31 CH-804, Zurich, Switzerland
41-1-492-61-30, 41-1-401-05-45 fax

Kitchen Arts and Letters
1435 Lexington Ave., New York, NY 10128.
(212) 876-5550.
Large store devoted to books on food and wine. Over
5,000 titles and free search service for out-of-print books.

The Pocket Doctor: Your Ticket to Good Health While Traveling
by Stephen Berushka, M.D.
Seattle: The Mountaineers, 1988

Spice Board of India
P.B. No: 1909, Cochin 682 018, India
91-484-353837, 91-484-364429 fax

*Trading Places: The Wonderful World of Vacation and Home
Exchanging* by Bill and Mary Barbour
Rutledge Hill Press, 1991

The Vacation Home and Hospitality Exchange Guide by John
Kimbrough
Kimco Communicatons, 1991.

Wilderness Cuisine by Carole Latimer
Berkeley, California: Wilderness Press, 1991
A gourmet trekkers' cookbook.

World Atlas of Wine by Hugh Johnson
New York: Simon & Schuster, 1971
Also deals with spirits.

Supplies

Emergency Essentials, Inc.
Orem, Utah.
(800) 999-1863
Catalog offering pre-packaged kits, bulk food, especially
dried food, MRE's, backpacker foods, dried staples, food
mills, canners, cookbooks.

Gevalia Coffee
(800) 438-4438
Fine coffee and paraphernalia for the road.

Nat Litt
House of Tea Ltd.
(215) 923-8327
Purveyors of the finest brick teas.

REI - Recreational Equipment, Inc.,
Sumner, Washington 98352-0001.
(800) 426-4840 (orders, US & Canada);
(206) 891-2500 (outside the US or Canada)
Over 70 listings for foods to take camping or hiking.

Military Combat Rations Providers

Right Away Foods
200 N. 1st St., McAllen, Texas

Canadian Commercial Corp/Freddy Inc.
50 Rue O'Conner St., Ottowa, Canada

Ary S.A.
Millington Drake
2049 Montevideor, Uruguay

International Food Processing
PO Box 230, Albert Park 3206, Victoria, Australia

BCB International LTD
Clydsmuir Road Industrial Estate, Cardiff CF2 2QS U.K.

Industrie Biscotti Crich, S.p.A.
31050 Zenson di Piave, Treviso, Italy

DIESE
264 Rue de Sables de Sary, 45770 Saran, France

Europavia Belgium, SA
Avenue des Courses 35, B1050 Brussels, Belgium

Oy Lunden Catering
Juhana Herttuan Puistokato 3, Fin-20200 Turku, Finland

House Swaps and Homestays

Friendship Force
Suite 575, South Tower, One CNN Ctr., Atlanta, GA 30303
(404) 522-9490

House Exchange Program
952 Virginia Ave., Lancaster, PA 17603
(717) 393-8985

Interhome
124 Little Falls Road, Fairfield, NJ 07004
(201) 882-6864

International Homestays Foreign Language/Study Abroad
Programs
Box 903, South Miami, FL 33143
(305) 662-1090

Intervac/International Home Exchange
Box 59054, San Francisco, CA 94519
(415) 435-3497

LEX Homestay in Japan/LEX America
68 Leonard Street, Belmont, MA 02178
(617) 489-5800

Servas
11 John Street, New York, NY 10038
(212) 267-0252

Vacation Exchange Club
Box 820, Hale'iwa, HI 96712
(800) 638-3841

Villas & Apartments Abroad, Ltd.
420 Madison Avenue, New York, N.Y. 10017
(212) 759-1025

WEB SITES

The World Wide Web offers a wealth of culinary resources to budding chefs and professional gourmands alike. From international recipes to personal restaurant reviews to food-minded travel leads—moveable feasts are at your fingertips. While the Internet is an invaluable tool, Web sites are constantly changing. We've found the following sites to be helpful or interesting, but it is by no means a comprehensive list on food and travel. Use it as a starting point. You will be pleased by the number of food lovers who congregate on the Internet and who are incredibly willing to share their knowledge and experience.

Bre World
http://www.breworld.com
BreWorld is Europe's largest Internet site dedicated to

the brewing industry. It lists international breweries, festivals, conferences, tastings, and awards.

Center for Food Safety & Applied Nutrition
http://vm.cfsan.fda.gov/list.html
CFSAN is a part of the Food and Drug Administration. For those who are concerned about food on the road, this site provides consumer information on food-borne illnesses and food safety.

CuisineNet
http://www.cuisinenet.com/
CuisineNet is great for adventure dining at home, domestically, or abroad. Complete with a restaurant guide for major U.S. cities, "Diner's Digest" reviews regional cooking, recipes, chefs, and food traditions from around the world, and "CuisineNet Live" features articles and chat rooms.

Diabetic Gourmet Magazine
http://www.gourmetconnection.com/diabetic
An offshoot of the Gourmet Connection, this Web site has valuable information on diabetic issues including: the latest news on drugs, advice, therapy, recipe exchanges, lifestyle forums, children with diabetes, and doctors. Click back to the Gourmet Connection an online magazine dedicated to gourmet food and health enthusiasts.

Diner's Grapevine
http://www.dinersgravepvine.com/
This site is a restaurant guide of almost 9,000 restaurants covering the Australia, Canada, France, Grand Cayman Islands, U.S., U.K., Venezuela, and the Virgin Islands.

Electronic Gourmet Guide
http://www.foodwine.com
A site to get excited about! Check out the regional recipes and the Global Gourmet Cookbook for an online collec-

tion of over 200 international recipes. The EGG also has daily food and wine features, shopping, a decent food-related links list, tips, columns, and much much more.

Epicurious Food
http://food.epicurious.com
This aesthetically sophisticated site doesn't do much with food and travel on its own, but is directly connected to *Condé Nast Traveler, Gourmet,* and *Bon Appétit.*

Fodor's Restaurant Index
http://www.fodors.com/ri.cgi
This site is excellent and what you would expect from Fodor's. While it's not the yellow pages for restaurants worldwide, you will find expert reviews of establishments that meet Fodor's standards for quality, service, and value.

Global Chef's World Recipes
http://www.swv.ie/recipe/index.htm
A site with recipes for you to create before leaving on a trip or to recreate after you have returned home.

GORP: Great Outdoor Recreation Pages
http://www.gorp.com/food
An old standby for all outdoor enthusiasts. They have a great food section that links and lists tips, recipes, books, and resources for cooking outdoors.

Gourmet World
http://www.gourmetworld.com/gw000002.htm
A one-stop shopping site of culinary references. You'll find links to worldwide chefs, restaurants, recipes, cooking schools, products and services, news, and entertainment.

International Food, Wine & Travel Writers Association
http://www.ifwtwa.org
The IFW&TWA is a prestigious organization. This site gives you basic information on membership and benefits,

how to apply, participation, and more. It is also a useful site for any traveler because it has a good list of pre-trip planning references such as: worldwide directories of chamber and commerces, city-states-provinces, tourist boards, convention and visitor's bureaus, telephone and zip codes, currency converters, airline weblinks, flight availability, weather forecasts, etc.

International Vegetarian Union
http://www.ivu.org
A multi-lingual collection of vegan recipes and vegetarian links from all parts of the world. One unique travel feature is a section on vegetarian phrases in different languages.

Internet Culinary Cyber City
http://www.culinary.net
This is a large site, but one nice feature is a section on travel and food called, "Forks in the Road."

World in your Kitchen
http://members.aol.com/WorldKitch/links.html
You'll enjoy the sections on International Cooking Sites, International Recipe Archives, and the Globe Trotter's Corner.

Vegetarian Pages
http://www.veg.org/veg
Check out the "World Guide to Vegetarianism," a listing of international vegetarian and vegetarian-friendly restaurants, stores, organizations, services, etc.

Vegetarian Resource Group
http://www.vrg.org/travel/index.htm
The VRG has a terrific Travel Section for vegetarian travelers. You'll find articles with topics such as "traveling with vegan children" and "business travel for vegetarians." They also have a great section called "Vegetarian Journal" with stories from globetrotting vegetarians.

$\mathcal{I}$NDEX OF
$\mathcal{C}$ONTRIBUTORS

ABOUT THE AUTHOR

Richard Sterling has been dubbed "The Indiana Jones of Gastronomy" by his admirers, and "Conan of the Kitchen" by *others*. He discovered the Way of the Fearless Diner when he was shipped off to the Far East as a teenage G.I. He is grateful to the Pentagon for the service. His other books include: *Dining with Headhunters; The Eclectic Gourmet Guide to San Francisco and the Bay Area;* and the award winning *Travelers' Tales Food: A Taste of the Road.* He is currently the travel editor of *Fiery Foods* magazine. He resides in Berkeley, California, where he is happy to be politically incorrect.

TRAVELERS' TALES
GUIDES

LOOK FOR THESE TITLES IN THE SERIES

GUTSY WOMEN
TRAVEL TIPS AND WISDOM FOR THE ROAD

By Marybeth Bond
ISBN 1-885211-15-5, 124 pages, $7.95

Packed with instructive and inspiring travel vignettes,
Gutsy Women: Travel Tips and Wisdom for the Road is a
must-have for novice as well as experienced travelers.

GUTSY MAMAS
TRAVEL TIPS AND WISDOM
FOR MOTHERS ON THE ROAD

By Marybeth Bond
ISBN 1-885211-20-1, 150 pages, $7.95

A book of tips and wisdom for mothers traveling with their
children. This book is for any mother, grandmother, son, or
daughter who travels or would like to.

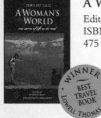

A WOMAN'S WORLD

Edited by Marybeth Bond
ISBN 1-885211-06-6
475 pages, $17.95

WINNER
BEST
TRAVEL
BOOK
LOWELL THOMAS AWARD

"I loved this book! From the very first story, I had
the feeling that I'd been waiting to read these
women's tales for years. I also had the sense that
I'd met these women before. I hadn't, of course,
but as a woman and a traveler I felt an instant
connection with them. What a rare pleasure."

—Kimberly Brown, *Travel & Leisure*

Check with your local bookstore for these titles or call O'Reilly to order:
800-998-9938 (credit cards only-Weekdays 6 AM–5 PM PST) 707-829-0515,
or email: order@oreilly.com

LOVE & ROMANCE
Edited by Judith Babcock Wylie
ISBN 1-885211-18-X, 294 pages, $17.95

"... a passion-filled tribute to the undeniable, inescapable romance of the road."
—Debra Birnbaum, Feature Editor, *New Woman*

A DOG'S WORLD
Edited by Christine Hunsicker
ISBN 1-885211-23-6, 232 pages, $12.95

"The stories are extraordinary, original, often surprising and sometimes haunting. A very good book."
—Elizabeth Marshall Thomas, author of
The Hidden Life of Dogs

THE ROAD WITHIN
Edited by Sean O'Reilly,
James O'Reilly & Tim O'Reilly
ISBN 1-885211-19-8, 443 pages, $17.95

"A revolutionary new style of travel guidebook."
— *New York Times News Service*

NEPAL
Edited by Rajendra S. Khadka
ISBN 1-885211-14-7, 423 pages, $17.95

"Always refreshingly honest, here is a collection that explains why Western travelers fall in love with Nepal and return again and again."
—Barbara Crossette, *New York Times* correspondent and author of *So Close to Heaven: The Vanishing Buddhist Kingdoms of the Himalayas*

FOOD
Edited by Richard Sterling
ISBN 1-885211-09-0, 444 pages, $17.95

SILVER MEDAL WINNER
BEST
TRAVEL
BOOK
LOWELL THOMAS AWARD

"Sterling's themes are nothing less than human universality, passion and necessity, all told in stories straight from the gut."
—Maxine Hong Kingston, author of
The Woman Warrior and *China Men*

BRAZIL

Edited by Annette Haddad & Scott Doggett
ISBN 1-885211-11-2, 433 pages, $17.95

"Only the lowest wattage dimbulb would visit Brazil without reading this book."
—Tim Cahill, author of *Jaguars Ripped My Flesh* and *Pecked to Death by Ducks*

SAN FRANCISCO

Edited by James O'Reilly,
Larry Habegger & Sean O'Reilly
ISBN 1-885211-08-2, 432 pages, $17.95

"As glimpsed here through the eyes of beatniks, hippies, surfers, 'lavender cowboys' and talented writers from all walks, San Francisco comes to vivid, complex life."
—*Publishers Weekly*

HONG KONG

Edited by James O'Reilly,
Larry Habegger & Sean O'Reilly
ISBN 1-885211-03-1, 438 pages, $17.95

"*Travelers' Tales Hong Kong* will order and delight the senses, and heighten the sensibilities, whether you are an armchair traveler or an old China hand."
—Gladys Montgomery Jones
Profiles Magazine, Continental Airlines

PARIS

Edited by James O'Reilly,
Larry Habegger & Sean O'Reilly
ISBN 1-885211-10-4, 424 pages, $17.95

"If Paris is the main dish, here is a rich and fascinating assortment of hors d'oeuvres. *Bon appetit et bon voyage!*"
—Peter Mayle

SPAIN

Edited by Lucy McCauley
ISBN 1-885211-07-4, 452 pages, $17.95

"A superb, eclectic collection that reeks wonderfully of gazpacho and paella, and resonates with sounds of heel-clicking and flamenco singing—and makes you feel that you are actually in that amazing state of mind called Iberia."
—Barnaby Conrad, author of *Matador* and *Name Dropping*

THAILAND

Edited by James O'Reilly & Larry Habegger
ISBN 1-885211-05-8, 405 pages, $17.95

"This is the best background reading
I've ever seen on Thailand!"
—Carl Parkes, author of *Thailand Handbook,
Southeast Asia Handbook* by Moon Publications

WINNER
BEST
TRAVEL
BOOK
LOWELL THOMAS AWARD

FRANCE

Edited by James O'Reilly,
Larry Habegger & Sean O'Reilly
ISBN 1-885211-02-3, 432 pages, $17.95

"All you always wanted to know about the French but were
afraid to ask! Explore the country and its people in a unique
and personal way even before getting there. Travelers' Tales:
your best passport to France and the French!"
—Anne Sengés, *Journal Français d'Amérique*

INDIA

Edited by James O'Reilly & Larry Habegger
ISBN 1-885211-01-5, 477 pages, $17.95

"The essays are lyrical, magical and evocative:
some of the images make you want to rinse
your mouth out to clear the dust."
—Karen Troianello, *Yakima Herald-Republic*

MEXICO

Edited by James O'Reilly & Larry Habegger
ISBN 1-885211-00-7, 426 pages, $17.95

"*Travelers' Tales Mexico* opens a window on the
beauties and mysteries of Mexico and the Mexicans. It's
entertaining, intriguing, baffling, instructive, insightful,
inspiring and hilarious—just like Mexico."
—Tom Brosnahan, coauthor of Lonely Planet's
Mexico – a travel survival kit

VISIT **TRAVELERS' TALES** ON THE WORLD WIDE WEB

http://www.oreilly.com/ttales

You'll discover which books we're working on, how to submit your own story, the latest writing contests you can enter, and the location of the next author event. We offer sample chapters from all of our books, as well as the occasional trip report and photo essay from our hard-working editors. Be sure to take one of our web tours, an exhaustive list of Internet resources for each of our titles, and begin planning your own journey.

SUBMIT YOUR OWN TRAVEL TALE

Do you have a tale of your own that you would like to submit to Travelers' Tales? We highly recommend that you first read one or more of our books to get a feel for the kind of story we're looking for. For submission guidelines and a list of titles in the works, send a SASE to:

Travelers' Tales Submission Guidelines
P.O. Box 610160, Redwood City, CA 94061

or send email to *ttguidelines@online.oreilly.com*
or check out our web site at **www.oreilly.com/ttales**

You can send your story to the address above or via email to *ttsubmit@oreilly.com*. On the outside of the envelope, *please indicate what country/topic your story is about*. If your story is selected for one of our titles, we will contact you about rights and payment.

We hope to hear from you. In the meantime, enjoy the stories!